Out of the Box and into the Frying Pan

Sermons Matter Series

Nicole Richardson

&

Parson's Porch Books

www.parsonsporchbooks.com

Out of the Box and into the Frying Pan

ISBN: Softcover 978-1-955581-57-8

Copyright © 2018 Nicole Richardson

Out of the Box and into the Frying Pan

Contents

Series Introduction

Parson's Porch Books is delighted to present to you this series called Sermons Matter.

We believe that many of the best writers are pastors who take the role of preacher seriously. Week in, and week out, they exegete scripture, research material, write and deliver sermons in the context of the life of their particular congregation in their given community.

We further believe that sermons are extensions of Holy Scripture which need to be published beyond the manuscripts which are written for delivery each Sunday. Books serve as a vehicle for the sermon to continue to proclaim the Good News of the Morning to a broader audience.

We celebrate the wonderful occasion of the preaching event in Christian worship when the Pastor speaks, the People listen and the Work of the Church proceeds.

Rev. Nicole Richardson provides us with an excellent example of an oral manuscript. When you read this book, you may think you are listening more than reading. Her sermons are winsome, yet serious, and simple, yet profound.

Take, Read, and Heed.

David Russell Tullock, M.Div., D.Min.
Publisher
Parson's Porch Books

What Would You Do for a Klondike Bar?

Genesis 25:19-34; Mark 6:1-13

What would you do for Klondike bar? Now, I imagine there are many of you who remember the commercial for that tasty ice cream treat calling people to think about what they would do for such a tasty treat. What would you do for a Klondike bar? I thought it was interesting that that slogan is still with us today, so I got on the internet and I did a little search to see what people today might do for a Klondike bar. I thought I would share a few of those with you. Someone said they would kiss a frog. Some said they'd bark like a dog. Others said that they would swim with sharks or wrestle with an alligator. Some like the idea that they would bungee jump from Mount Rushmore for a Klondike bar. I thought this person was a little more adventurous, a little more on the edge; he said he would go streaking through Walmart. This one is my favorite; this person said he would be willing to tip over porta potties. Yeah, I know. A little messy, a little dangerous, a little risky what some of these people have in their mind for what they would do for a Klondike bar.

During this last week, one of the youth here at the church sent me a little bumper sticker on Facebook. I thought it was the perfect bumper sticker; it said I'm haunted by the things I did for a Klondike bar. I'm haunted by the things I did for a Klondike bar.

I imagine that might be something that was going through Esau's and maybe even Jacob's mind after they kind of lived through this story that we find in Genesis. This story startswith a big line of confrontation and conflict with families; the nations of this faith of ours. It starts in an innocent sort of way. Here is Esau, he is a man of the outdoors, and he works out in a field tending flocks. Jacob,

9

he remains quiet and at home. After a long day of working out in the field, Esau comes in and we discover that he is famished. It just so happens that Jacob is located right on the path as Esau's coming in. He's been cooking up some stew. Esau comes up and says, "give me some of your stew my brother." "Give me some of your stew." Well, Jacob being the enterprising fellow that he says, "Okay I'll give you some of my stew, but only if you promise to give me your birthright; only if you give me your birthright." "Yes, yes I'll give it to you!" "No, no, no! Swear to me that I have it!" Esau swears, and in the end, Esau ends up grabbing a hold of the Klondike Bar.

He's willing to give up his inheritance, his birthright, for the immediacy of his needs. His hunger took a hold of him and he was willing to give up his security, his prosperity, and a double portion of Isaac's inheritance that would go to him because he is the oldest son. He's willing to give it away for a Klondike bar. I imagine Esau pondered those things that haunted him because he was willing to sell his birthright. I mean here was Jacob who was willing to go after what he wanted; to find a way to manipulate Esau so that Jacob himself could have what his older brother had, and he didn't. He was willing to scheme and devise a plan to take something away from his kin. I imagine too that he may be haunted by his actions to grab a hold of his Klondike Bar. The people in Jesus's hometown, how about them?

They were not willing to grab a hold of the inheritance, the birthright, that grew up amongst them and instead they rejected him, unwilling to accept that the kingdom of God may be present in this one that they knew. What birthright, what inheritance, has God placed in your hands, in our hands as the body of Christ? What has God placed in our hands? Are we on the verge possibly of selling it, selling our birthright, for a Klondike bar? It's not an easy sort of place to be because our culture, our society has a way of tempting us and luring us away from the things that God places in us to take care of, to nurture, to allow for the kingdom of God to be known. While we were in Jamaica with the senior high youth a couple weeks ago, we were blessed by meeting Pastor Leroy Blackwood. He is the pastor of the Victory Christian Fellowship. The church that we were called to be present with, to do vacation bible school, and to help with some construction. We had the blessing of sitting down with him early Monday morning and he shared his story with us. He shared with us that when he was growing up, he didn't really have a mother and his father wasn't a great role model.

He had no shoes, only one outfit, and he often went hungry. There was no indoor plumbing, no air conditioning, no refrigeration, the restroom was outside, and life was very difficult. When he was a young boy, he started attending a church and he grabbed a hold of his faith. He claimed that in that moment, he finally was saved. God showed him what his inheritance, his birthright, was. God placed in him a vision that called him to start a church in Jamaica for the people that needed to hear God's Word. It was a risky sort of venture.

He had no money and he wasn't sure how to make it happen, but he did. He pressed forward on this vision God placed in him and he grabbed a hold of his inheritance and moved forward. He said that the first Sunday had only seven people. The second Sunday had fourteen people and it just grew. Now, it wasn't something that didn't have its challenges. He said the church in which he had found his faith, he learned that women weren't allowed to wear slacks, jewelry, or makeup.

God gave him another experience. Pastor Leroy ended up in another church and he discovered that were other churches and other ways of accepting people. He found that the women of this church could wear pants, wear jewelry, and makeup. He thought that this is more about who the kingdom of God is, and he allowed that to be a part of his congregation. Now, the challenge was when the people from the other church where he was nurtured and found his faith, came to him and said, "Pastor Leroy, what are you thinking?" "We've taught you better." "You need to have the women refrain from dressing in such ways."

He could have been thrown off track by those who wanted the church structured how they envisioned it but he stayed on the course. Now, that's not the only struggle that came along his path. He eventually married and had children.

The problem was that he didn't have enough money to provide for his family. They didn't have enough food, clothes, and they really didn't have a place to live. This became a huge burden because he should be providing for his family, yes? There was a group that came along and told him they'd like to buy his church.

He told his wife that they'd been offered money for this group to buy the church and he asked her what she thought about it. She said, "well, this isn't my calling." "God did not place this vision in my head." "The choice is yours." He thought well darn it! He was hoping she would give him the easy answer. He wrestled and prayed, and he realized that if he would've sold his church, he would've been just like Esau. He would've sold his inheritance, his birthright, to grab a hold of the Klondike bar.

It's not an easy thing but it's also the truth of our relationship with God and the journey of faith and what Jesus calls us to. He says to the disciples as he sends them out, "don't take any money, don't take any food, don't take any extra clothing." You think, man that Jesus is a little difficult! What if we don't find any food, any shelter, and what if it gets cold at night? The truth that Jesus speaks to is that aspect of risk, of trusting God with the provision for our journey. It is very easy for us to be pulled off the path.

It's very easy for us to grab a hold of the Klondike bar that may be offered to us to keep us from moving forward with the vision that

God has placed in us. Like Pastor Leroy, maybe there are people that are trying to convince you that things should look different. Perhaps there are institutions or others that convince you that you have no other choice. Perhaps you moved forward with the vision and the results just don't seem to be what you thought they'd be and disappointment can lead us away from our inheritance. What is the inheritance, the vision, that God has placed in you?

What is the inheritance that God has placed in us here at First Presbyterian? Are we grabbing a hold of the inheritance? Are we taking the opportunity to take risks, and to trust that God goes with us and God provides, and we will not perish? Pastor Leroy told the group he couldn't sell his church, his birthright. A couple of months later, Mission Discovery found Pastor Leroy.

They engaged in relationship with Pastor Leroy and now he's been able to start three churches. He's now able to feed his family and Mission Discovery helped to put a roof over his family's head. The risk that Pastor Leroy took, the trust that he stepped out on, gives us hope that if we are obedient and faithful with what God has entrusted us with, God will not leave us alone. What about us? Are we willing to grab a hold of the vision, of our inheritance, and run head long into the future or are we going to take a little bite of the Klondike bar? I believe in the God who walks with us, the one who is faithful and trustworthy, the one who won't let us stumble. The challenge is in front of us. I pray that in the end, we won't be the ones saying, "I'm haunted by the things I did for the Klondike bar." Amen.

How Can We Belong If We Can't Find Our Place?

Mark 1:29-39

Belonging; I believe that it is one of the deepest human gut sort of needs. I think this need to belong has really been at the heart of so much angst that occurs in our world. There's so much angst, so much hurt, so much pain, only because someone or a group of people want to belong. You see, belonging, that need to belong, that hunger to belong, is about not being alone, being in community, being in a place where there is a level of intimacy. I'm talking about the intimacy that comes when we sit with people that love us no matter who we are, and we love them back.

I think this core human desire to belong really drives us back to Genesis when God is creating. In one of those creation stories, we hear God created Adam. Do you remember what we hear? We hear it's not good for him to be alone. God saw that it was not good for a human being to be alone. No man ought to be an island. There is something about connectedness, relationship, community, and intimacy that drives what God is all about. We continue with the theme from last week. Simon's mother-in-law is sick with a high fever and we know that in Jesus's time, that being sick is an isolating event. Whether it's leprosy, cancer, or demon possession, being sick keeps one from being in community and from belonging.

That is one of the big pieces of this kingdom of God that Mark is trying to communicate with these stories of what Jesus is all about. A lot of times we get stuck on this notion that it's all about the healing that Jesus does. If we get stuck on that, we miss the Gospel message that Mark is trying to communicate. As we hear later in this reading, after Jesus has done a lot of healing in the neighborhood, he goes off to pray. Peter, Simon, Andrew, and the cohorts go to Jesus and tell him that people are looking for him to heal them. They say, "come on Jesus, you're doing great and you could start your own franchise maybe!" Jesus recognizes that when the people are motivated by healing, they miss the message of God. Healing for the sake of healing isn't what God is about! As difficult of a truth as that may be, that's not what the Gospel is about! Jesus heals because it's about wholeness, community, and it's about the proclamation. If we think it's just about the healing and not about what it means to be in community with each other, we've missed the point of the Gospel.

It's not about us. It's about the greater good, the kingdom of God, the proclamation and one other piece that we see in the story. We don't know if Simon's mother-in-law is the one fixing the meals and taking care of everyone. All we know is that she is down and out, isolated from the family because she is sick. Jesus lifts her up, touches her, and she is healed. In that healing, she finds her place. She gets up and she serves. She gets up and she is ministering to the people that are gathered there, including Jesus. She finds her place in the act of Jesus bringing her back into the community, back into belonging. She does something very significant.

It's the Sabbath and what were Jews not supposed to do on the Sabbath? They're not supposed to cook, clean, or do any work on the Sabbath. Yet, Simon's mother-in-law serves and changes that dynamic of this idea that healing is for the sake of healing. It's healing for the sake of serving, ministry, and communicating this discipleship. This woman is the first disciple and she did it because she found where her place was, and that place was in the kingdom of God. This place in the kingdom of God that comes from intimacy, from touch, is profound. The other aspect of that is that it reminds us who God is. God knew that it wasn't right for man to be alone. God knew that it took intimacy and risk. So much so that he risked his son to be born, raised, loved, and nurtured by human beings.

God knows the importance of intimacy and vulnerability for community to be built. Today, we take another step in discipleship and in creating a space for people to belong. As we allow Jesus to change our hearts, those hearts changed lead us to do what Jesus said to Simon and the cohorts. "We're not going back to heal or do miracles." "We're going to another town to preach the kingdom of God." That's why Jesus came and that's why we are here. We're here to take this Word, and this sense of belonging to help our world and community to be transformed and understand that each and every one of us belong. Today, in the biggest act of intimacy, we celebrate this meal. A meal that Jesus sat down and broke bread, poured the cup, and offered himself so that all of us could understand what it means to belong. Today, we celebrate the Lord's Supper together with God and for his kingdom. Let us come together and know deeply and profoundly what it means to belong and know our part. Amen.

And the Kingdom Can Be Yours If the Price is Right!

Isaiah 58:1-9; Matthew 5:13-16

How many of you like to win stuff? I like to win stuff. You know it'd be nice if I could win a big pile of money. Maybe a new car because our cars seem to never work very well. Maybe you all would like to win new toys or a new Gameboy, or a new computer. We like to win stuff, don't we? Well, how can we win the kingdom of God? Well, in this world we live in, it's very clear that to have stuff, you win, right? We are driven by having stuff, winning stuff, getting ahead in this world.

The other side of that is that we've also heard that we really don't need to be religious, and we don't need God because all we need to do is do good things. How many of you have heard people say, "I don't need to be a person of faith because I do good things in this world." "Since I do good things, I probably do more than those people who claim to be Christian, right?" Well, Christians on the other hand, we sort of have bought into this notion in this world. If we're honest, we've bought into this notion of the things we do and if we do enough good things, enough committee meetings, enough mission trips, and be nice to our neighbors, we'll have the right price for the kingdom of God.

It's kind of like as people of faith, we look at faith as kind of a fire insurance. Fire insurance; it saves us from the burning fires of hell! We cannot mislead ourselves that if we come to worship every Sunday, we will have a great big positive checkmark of gold stars in the kingdom of heaven and we've got it made. We can't do enough good things to earn that gold star either. That's the trick of faith, so to speak. It's not a works righteousness path. To be light in the world, it takes more than being a great attender in worship, serving on committee meetings, or serving in sessions. It takes more than just doing stuff. Isaiah says, "God doesn't care about our fasting, our sacrifices, or how many times we end up in worship if our lives are devoid of a deep relationship with God." It is in that deep relationship with God, that propels us to do the things that are about the kingdom of God. Jesus says to the disciples and the people that are sitting around listening, "you are to be the salt in the world and you are to be the light in the world" but those things aren't solely about doing good deeds.

It has more to do with what is in your heart, what is the intention with which you engage in worship and how you engage the ministry that God has placed in your hands. If we don't have an intention in our heart and in our spirit at being first in relationship with God and one another, all the things we do really have no worth. Now, the other thing about God is that God isn't a linear sort of God. He doesn't really go from point A to B to C to D in a nice straight line. He's really kind of cyclical in nature and when God calls us to be salt and light, he then follows that up with what sounds like an if then statement. That's how we get sort of trapped when we look at these things as if then statements. We get trapped by the if then statement that means that we must do good things and be at church on Sunday even if we're not really worshiping. We must do those things to be salty, but I think this is where the trick is in God. It isn't the typical if then statement.

The reality is that Jesus says," we are salt." The truth is that salt is one of the most stable compounds we have. We can set it out in one of our containers and it never loses its saltiness. The only way salt starts to lose some of its saltiness is when it's dissolved in water. The truth is we are salt. The if then piece only comes into recognizing that we are salt. If we don't even recognize that we are salt, how can we be salty in this world? That if then statement is more about being aware that we have this calling to be salt and to be light in this world.

He's really kind of speaking in a confrontational sort of way without really being confrontational. Salt; it's a symbol of covenant. It is of hospitality and it was used to clean babies, as an antiseptic, and for flavoring. It was understood as fidelity, purity, and non-corruption. If salt represents all of these things, then it means that's what it means for us to be salt. He said, "we are to be light in the world." We are light. Not maybe you'll be light if you do enough things. It doesn't matter who you are, where you are, what age you are, right? You and I are called to be light and to shine! The only way we can do these things is by absorbing and engaging in worship and bringing ourselves to God in an intention that means that we really, really want to mean this and we really, really want to be in a relationship! We must be open to absorbing light and to being rocks painted with glow in the dark paint.

The kingdom can be yours if the price is right. The price is right. The funny thing is today we celebrate communion, right? This thing right here that we do indicates to us that the price that is right is sacrifice. God knew what the price for his kingdom was and he paid it. He gave us the kingdom and that price was at the cost of the death of his own son. The kingdom has already been won by us. The question is do we really, really want it? Do we really want to be salt and light in this world? If we do, it calls us to the same kind of sacrifice that God was willing to give for us. This is a table of joy and hope but it's also a table that challenges us to be in relationship with God, with one another, and in this world in ways that really challenge us to sacrifice what we want, what we desire. When we get to that place where we're willing to sacrifice all that to have the kingdom that's already there for us, we will be amazed at what God has for us. The kingdom can be yours if the price is right. The price has been offered up. Will we receive it? Amen.

Closet Full of Fig Leaves

Genesis 2:15-17; 3:1-7; Matthew 4:1-11

How many of you really know what the season of Lent is all about? Raise your hand. Sort of; we have some who know. We do this season every church year and unfortunately, we don't set ourselves up to really help us journey during Lent in a way that we really ought to be doing. You see, Lent is this time that we recognize that Jesus spent forty days and forty nights in the desert. That's what this time of Lent is about. It's about this desert journey. It's a time to contemplate what it means that Jesus was preparing himself in all his humanness to confront his ministry that God was calling him to. It's a time for us to walk in the same desert and to confront our humanness so that we can be prepared for what God calls us to. It's a time to reflect on our brokenness and the ways in which we fall short of who God has created us to be. It's a serious season. It's a season of contemplation, reflection, meditation, and of looking at ourselves with honesty.

These Scriptures really call us to that kind of reflection and journey. This story in the Garden of Eden is quite profound. The first eleven chapters of Genesis are considered a primeval sort of dissertation on God's part on who we are as human beings, and to get at the truth of our relationships with each other and God. Chapter three calls us to reflect on how we have fallen from God's grace. How many of you have heard this story called The Fall? We've been told this is the story of disobedience many times.

I think on the top level; the sin of disobedience is what this story is about. I think it is about so much more than that though. It really calls us to look at how easily we tend to go after what our ego desires. See there they were, Adam and Eve, and the snake shows up and says, "did God say that you couldn't eat from this fruit?" Eve says, "we can eat from any other tree other than this one in the middle, this tree of the knowledge of the good and bad." Eve says, "we can't eat from it or even touch it."

God doesn't say they can't touch it, but Eve adds this because she knows how much of a temptation it is. The snake says, "no, you're not going to die but God doesn't want you to eat because then you'll know good and bad and you'll be like God." "God doesn't want you to be like him." The snake speaks to that inner core of our ego and tempts us and says, "God is a God to be mistrusted." "God is not fully gracious, and he doesn't want you to be like him." If we're honest and place ourselves in Eve's shoes, we probably would have the same response. That's right! God must be mistrusted, and he is trying to keep something from us, and what kind of God doesn't want us to be like him?

Our ego, our desires to be like God and have that power and control, that's where our brokenness lies. It's not as much about the disobedience as it as about our willingness to be tweaked by what the snake has to say. How many of you have seen the movie, *Bruce Almighty*? It came out in the early 2000's and it's such a fun movie! "Smite me almighty Smiter!" He's so aggravated with God who keeps him from having success. He's like "God is like a kid with a magnifying glass and I'm an ant and he's frying off my antlers!" It is how we respond when God doesn't give us what we want.

We're back in the garden and the snake is tempting us once again and saying you really want to be like God. If we're like God, the truth of the matter is we don't need God anymore. That's the real sin, folks! The real downfall is that we separate ourselves from God every time we enter that Garden of Eden! When we separate, we miss out. There's a death and when you eat from that tree of knowledge of good and bad, there's a death of your innocence. We have a difficulty of letting go of that power and control. As soon as Adam and Eve ate, their eyes were open and what happened? They recognized that they were naked! That visual image of being naked really calls us to our recognition of being vulnerable. What do they do because they're naked? They hide but what else do they do? They sew clothes with fig leaves to cover themselves up.

We tend to keep our vulnerability from God and others because then we look weak and we're not like God. We have a closet full of fig leaves that we put on every single day. The problem is when that mistrust seeps in, it leads to fear. Fear leads to what? More fear and hate. Hate leads to what? Suffering! We have people who are willing to take others out because of their fear and mistrust of groups of people. It's one of the things that's at the heart of what happened to the Indian man who was shot in Kansas a week and a half ago. A guy was driven by mistrust, leading to hate, and hate leading to suffering. He didn't even know the nationality or ethnicity of the man he killed.

When we're driven by our ego, our desire to be like God, and put on our fig leaves, we end up creating a world of suffering. Jesus showed us in his own temptations, that the snake approached Jesus and challenged Jesus to take control of his ego and have the power. Jesus refused to take a hold of that power and control even if it satisfied his own good. If you watch *Bruce Almighty*, he gets the power and he is God and he goes after what satisfies him. He even uses it to try to destroy a newscaster's life, right?

This journey shows us that there is something bigger than ourselves. If we're going to enter Lent, we need to be aware of the fig leaves that we put on, so we can take them off, and be vulnerable and not mistrust God. You have a fig leaf in your bulletin and I want you to be honest with yourself and honest with God. What things are you afraid to let God know about you? What are the fig leaves that you put on? What ways do you keep yourself from being vulnerable to God? Then, I want you to write on your fig leaves, what ways do you keep yourself from being vulnerable from the people sitting around you? If we can remove these fig leaves, we will journey in a much deeper way through Lent. We will be the kingdom that God calls us to be if we're honest! We can be clearer in our journey of discipleship. I want you take that fig leaf with you and keep it as a reminder for ways to remove the fig leaves from your closet so that when we get to Easter, we'll be more fully known by God, by each other, and by ourselves. I hope you'll be able to say yes to this question by the end of the season. Are you ready to purge your closet of fig leaves? Amen.

BYOB: Bring Your Own Bone

Ezekiel 37:1-14; Luke 24:13-22

How many of you have read the entire book of Ezekiel? We have a couple, right? Ezekiel isn't really a pretty book, is it? It is full of images of destruction and death. With God, all things are possible. Ezekiel is called by God to do strange things. Things that don't seem to make sense in our hearts. What was Ezekiel called to do when his wife died? With God, all things are possible! He was called to not grieve. He wasn't allowed to grieve. With God, all things are possible! I liken the imagery of the valley of the dried bones to what we see in our culture. How many of you watch TV and have watched *CSI*, *NCIS*, or *The Walking Dead*? There's also a show called, *Bones*, right? We are fascinated just in our TV realm with death and destruction.

This is the context in which we hear this story. Our fascination with death in Ezekiel should be highly tuned to the society and culture that we live in today. Here is Ezekiel, prophet of God, who was called by God and carried to a valley to see bones. There is a huge valley of bones, dead people, and they have been there for a while. They're not rotting anymore. They are brittle and have been picked dry by the birds of the air and animals of the field.

God calls Ezekiel to prophesy to these dry bones. Now a little background;, the reason that Ezekiel was full of death, is because the Southern Kingdom of Israel had been taken off into exile by the Babylonians, right? King David and King Solomon had a united kingdom and after King Solomon's death, there was civil unrest and it was split into the Northern and Southern Kingdom. The Northern Kingdom was hauled off into exile by the Assyrians. About two hundred years later, the Southern Kingdom fell. The reason these kingdoms fell was because the people of Israel lost their way. They had lost their understanding of what it means to be in relationship with God. Their worship had grown dry, brittle, dead, and they were full of themselves. They were living in ways that were completely destructive to God's will. There was a lot of killing, adultery, child sacrifice, and love of money that drew them away from God. God pulled them into exile and this is the context of Ezekiel. The death, the dry bones, the symbol that Israel was dead. I have been in that dead place. Have you all been in that dead place? Is our church in that dead place? I want to believe that this community isn't quite in a completely dead place.

The truth is, we must be honest with ourselves in how we engage life, God, our worship and what we are called to do to show this world that we aren't dead! See the thing is, that in this world, in our community, in this place, in this time, people are hungry for something! People are wanting something that gives them life and sustenance! If we're honest, as a community, they don't see us providing anything to feed their hunger or to help them feel a sense of purpose! If we look around, we are dead to the people who aren't' here. Do you doubt me? There is so much pain and hurt all around.

We have racism, sexism, and ageism. We've got so many people that are angry and fearful, and they are looking for a way to find hope. I guarantee it, they don't' see the church as a place to find that! Ezekiel comes to this valley of dry bones and God says, "prophesy to these dry bones and tell them they will no longer be dead!" There was a great scene and they were still not alive, and God says, "prophesy again!" "Tell them I will breathe life into you and they will no longer be dead!" The question is in this Scripture., Do we want our hearts burning inside of us? Do we want a sense of hope? Do we want to be alive again making a difference?

The truth is that we can't keep doing this! This is not giving life to those who are hungry! If the world sees us as dead, we are good for no one. We must decide today who we are going to serve! We have to decide today if we want to be transformed and to be lifted out of our graves and have God's breath put back in us in a new and profound way! You see, those bones were dry and brittle and the point of that is there is no hope when you look at the valley of dry bones! Do you believe in a God that can bring life out of death? Do you? If we do believe in a God that can bring life out of dry bones, why are we so reluctant to be transformed?

My guess is because transformation means we have to give up things that we hold dear. Change means that we must trust that whatever change is going to do to us is going to be for the better. We must find a way to connect with the community around us. The mission field isn't just across oceans, it's right outside our doors. We must have the courage to engage in relationships. I do believe that God wants us to be in relationships with the people down the street, next door, across the street, people you work with, and go to school with and engage them as human beings.

God knows when we engage each other with love and compassion and equality, we are changed. We are transformed. That breath that God asked Ezekiel to prophesy into the dry bones is the same breath that God offers us when we allow ourselves to be in relationships with others and engage in their ickiness. It also allows them to engage in our ickiness. Just because we're Christians doesn't mean we have it figured out, and it doesn't mean we don't have ickiness anymore.

There are still a lot of you that haven't signed up for the Seder meal and this is an opportunity to engage with the Rainbow School. I'll give you one more day to sign up. Darron Story is the newest elder and he is responsible for mission and outreach. You know what? If you expect Darron to do it all so that you can feel the breath of life of God filling you, you've completely missed the point of what God has to say today. We need to be asking God how do we connect with the communities around us? We need to be recognizing that no matter how old we are, no matter how frail our bones are, there are ways to engage with people and to be changed by God. When we allow God's breath to fill us and bring us to life, people are drawn to that energy. If people are drawn to us, they will find this is no longer a graveyard of dead people.

They will find that this is a place where God is living, moving, and using us and they want to be a part of it. The disciples on the way to Emmaus were sad because their hopes, their dreams of what Jesus was going to be about were dead. They didn't even recognize him until they sat down at the table, and he broke bread and their eyes were open. It is around meal, around community, around fellowship that God can be tasted and known. That's what we do today. We come to this table to have our hopes and dreams that were dead brought back to life. Do you as individuals want to have new life? Are you honest with me? Do we as a people of God want God to breathe new life into us? I expect no more pushback then in how we're going to relate to people.

Communion is a celebration, a party! God invites us to bring our own dead bones to the party. We are all invited to bring our dead bones to the table of God because with God, all things are possible! With God, all things are possible! Amen.

As the Topsy-Turvy World Turns

Matthew 21: 1-11; 12-17

Which kingdom would you likely find yourself in? If you were in Jesus's time in Jerusalem, which kingdom would you find yourself in? Scholars have discovered that on the day that Jesus was coming into Jerusalem, there was another entry into Jerusalem on the other side of the city. Did you all know that?

Jesus came in from the east and on that very same day, on the west side of Jerusalem, Pilate was coming into town. Pilate was coming into town not on a donkey or a colt, not with disciples, people looking for healing, or people throwing palm branches or their coats on the ground.

Pilate came in on a mounted horse, followed by armies of people in their army gear with spears and shields. He came in with power and might, and in that arrival, he declared what kingdom had control and power? Rome, right?

Yet, on the other side of Jerusalem, came a man not covered with armor, not with a band of armies with spears and shields, not on strong and steady horses. He came with a little donkey and a colt. He came proclaiming a different kingdom. He came proclaiming not a kingdom of money, power, and control but a kingdom that would bring healing and wholeness, a healing of forgiveness.

A kingdom that turns this world's understanding upside down of what it means to love, to be in power, to risk, and to sacrifice. Things that the other kingdom couldn't even begin to comprehend. Let me ask you again; when it comes to the reality of the kingdom that you live in, the concerns that are in your hearts, the anxieties that consume us as a people of faith, do we live in the kingdom that Jesus brings in that Palm Sunday or do we live as though we live in the kingdom of Rome? It's a hard question to ask us but it must be asked today! You see, on this day, we should be excited about the kingdom, this man called Jesus and what he offers and proclaims that God is all about! We should be shouting hosannas! We should be singing this is the day that the Lord has made! Let us rejoice and be glad in it!

We should but you realize that those same people that were following Jesus, waving palm branches, and throwing coats on the road, were the very ones that said crucify him. Those same people in four to five short days turned on him and were no longer saying hosanna, thank God you're here but now were saying crucify him! It begs the question, what happened? What happened that in four to five short days, those people could so quickly turn their focus?

The next story that I read is the story of Jesus going to the temple where the people of the Jewish faith make their sacrifices and give their honor to God. He tears up everything and throws it upside down! I'll bet you a whole year's salary that this one act is the thing that caused Jesus to get killed. If we're under any illusion that we're not offended that Jesus came in and turned these things upside down, we are fooling ourselves.

This means that Jesus confronts our little kingdoms, even our church. He comes in and says, "those of you who think you have it all figured out and under control, you're fooling yourselves." He says, "the longer that you cheat the people, the longer that you lead the people astray, the longer that you don't let your world be turned upside down, the more difficult it will be to understand, conceive, and embrace the kingdom God has."

We have to admit that we can easily be a part of that crowd that shouts crucify him four days later! Guess what, we have this journey ahead of us and if I don't see you Maundy Thursday and Good

Friday living out our story and admitting these pieces of who we are and what it means to be people of faith, I'll be incredibly disappointed! Maundy Thursday; the night that Jesus shares with the disciples and washes their feet. He humbles himself as the king and washes their dirty, nasty, icky feet. He sits at that table with Judas and Judas soon betrays him. Then we get to Good Friday and we live that darkness out. We recognize our fickleness, our ways that easily turn us from hosannas to crucify him and put him on that freaking cross!

There is no way, saints, we can get through the week to next Sunday, Easter Sunday, and not go through this pain and suffering. Easter means absolutely nothing without that! We have been called to this place, this community, to do the work that takes us from hosannas to the cross. If you choose to take a seat in the kingdom of Jesus, in God's kingdom, it means a lot of work and sacrifice. It means putting yourself and your desires, our desires, this community's desires, and putting it over here. It means living out what it is that God wants us to do and wants us to be.

No matter how much we like worship the way we like it, not that you all are prone to that, but you understand the truth to that, right? We cannot remain there anymore. God did not come in Jesus in a beautiful palace. He came in Jesus in a manger. God did not come to continue to support suppression, oppression, and subjugation. He did not come to use power and might to bring about unity. He came with humbleness, challenge, and love. Tell me if you recognize this; Mary said;

My soul glorifies the Lord
    and my spirit rejoices in God my Savior,
    for he has been mindful
    of the humble state of his servant.

From now on all generations will call me blessed,
  for the Mighty One has done great things for me—
  holy is his name.

His mercy extends to those who fear him,
  from generation to generation.

He has performed mighty deeds with his arm;
  he has scattered those who are proud
  in their inmost thoughts.

He has brought down rulers from their thrones
  but has lifted up the humble.

He has filled the hungry with good things
  but has sent the rich away empty.

He has helped his servant Israel,
  remembering to be merciful
  to Abraham and his descendants forever,
  just as he promised our ancestors.

These words are Mary's song, the mother of Jesus when she found out she was pregnant and goes to her cousin Elizabeth. Do you all remember now? These words are prophetic words and they speak of the Son and what he is going to be about. He is going to turn our institutions, corporations, our families, our churches upside down, topsy-turvy. Do we believe that God has a plan? Do we believe that the God that turns things all wonky and upside down has a plan? Jesus comes even now on a donkey without any protection. Which kingdom will we find ourselves in this week? As the topsy-turvy worlds turns, may God turn us upright once more. Amen.

Every Scar Tells a Story

Genesis 32:22-31; Matthew 8:1-4

Have you ever found yourself between a rock and a hard place? I have multiple times over found myself between that rock and hard place. Honestly, I probably did it to myself. What about you? Yeah! That is where we find Jacob today. Last week, we heard the story of how Jacob wanted to get a hold of his older brother's Esau's inheritance.

In this time, the oldest child would receive the father's inheritance. Jacob wanted that inheritance so badly that he was willing to manipulate his older brother out of that inheritance. If we follow his story to where we are, there's seven chapters that transpire and in that time, we hear how Jacob manipulated his older brother out of his inheritance. We also hear that their mother convinced Jacob to trick his father into giving him the inheritance and blessing Jacob. That verbal blessing was supposed to be for Esau as well. His mother told Jacob to put on some fur because Esau was a hairy man, and his father was blind and so he could be easily fooled. That is what Jacob did. He's a friendly sort of fellow, right?

He found out that Esau was so angry that Esau wanted to kill him. Rebecca told Jacob to run away and he ends up staying with his mother's family. He works for Laban, who ends up being his father-in-law. Jacob gets a taste of his own trickery when Laban tricks him into marrying off both of his daughters. He works, and he finally gets to a point where he's so tired of working for Laban, that he runs away. We catch up with Jacob in this story and he's in between a rock and a hard place because of his own doing. He told Laban that he's not going to work for him anymore, so he can't return. He also finds out that he can't move forward because Esau is still out for vengeance and Esau has a troop of four-hundred. He's in a desperate place. I've kind of been there. Jacob realizes that his choices have caused his past catch up with him. He does what he can. He sends off a huge gift to his brother hoping to appease his brother. He splits off and tries to protect his family. Then he is so tired and it's time to sleep. That is where God finally shows up and meets him face to face.

God comes, and God is the initiator of this wrestling. Jacob doesn't say, "hey guy, let's have a WWE moment." God is the one who comes to Jacob and says, "it is time to wrestle." There is great psychological wrestling going on. God faces off in a wrestling match with Jacob to see if he is actually willing to fess up to that sin. How many of us, if we met with God in a wrestling match, really want to fess up to our sin? I mean we do a confession of sin every Sunday but I'm guessing I'm not the only one sitting in this camp.

I think that I'm basically a good Christian. I don't murder anyone, and I don't tell lies, at least not any really big lies. I haven't really stolen anything, but I think I did steal a pack of gum when I was a little girl. Despite all those things, I still think I'm a good Christian. I'm not that bad. How about all of you? When we start evaluating our own goodness, and how holy we are, we have a hard time looking at our own ego and our refusal to really submit to God. I think that's the wrestling match that's going on with God! God could've ended that wrestling match at any time, but he continued to wrestle with Jacob all night. I think that's what God really does with us! He really wants us to figure out how to submit earlier.

We must recognize that if we are in control, then God is not the one in the driver's seat. God finally realized that Jacob was going to wrestle and wrestle and not fess up to his sin, so God did something impressive. He zapped Jacob in the thigh and crippled him. It's a great sort of visual and emotional symbolism there. Jacob no longer has the capacity to run away from God or run away from his sin because he is now a crippled man. God finally stops Jacob in the tracks and tells Jacob that he'll give him one more chance. Jacob wants the blessing, but he can't get the blessing from God until he fesses up to God. Jacob finally has an honest moment with God. God asks him what is your name? At that time, names had meaning. Jacob finally admitted who he is. He said, "I am the heel grabber, the Supplanter, the one who schemes and manipulates." Would we be as courageous to actually admit our real, deep name to God? That is the challenge of being able to face our sin.

The passage that we read from Matthew earlier is really the recognition of that very thing. At that time, leprosy was considered the result of one's sin. Those who had leprosy were shunned because they had sinned. They weren't allowed to interact with other people and does anybody know what they had to do if they came around clean people? They had to shout "unclean" and ring a bell that the unclean were coming through. Here in that story in Matthew, this leper, he came right up to Jesus and said to Jesus, "if you will Jesus, you can heal me." That leper was saying to Jesus, "I recognize my sin, but you can heal me." Jesus did just that.

Jesus recognized the isolation one has in their sin and this leper desired to be restored and to be brought back into the community. The challenge for us even in this day is to admit that we find ourselves between a rock and a hard place and we do it to ourselves. The way out to receive that blessing is to admit that we are broken and admit the scars that come along on the journey because of the way we have broken the relationships with ourselves, with our families, with strangers, and with this world. We need to be like Jacob and have the courage to admit our name, our brokenness, our scars, and then have a story to tell the world.

Instead of being ashamed, let us approach God's throne like that leper. Let us admit the ways in which we fall short, to admit the ways in which we separate ourselves from ourselves, from one another, from ultimately God. Jacob admitted that name but God didn't leave him there. God doesn't just zap him and say, "you're own your own!" Names mean something so important that Jacob is renamed to Israel. Israel meaning you have wrestled God, human beings, and yourself and you have prevailed. This is a huge name change and blessing.

If we have the courage and tenaciousness, God will bless us, change our name, and move us into a new place so that we can tell these scar stories and how good God is. Let us approach that throne with courage. Today, we celebrate communion together in that very testimony of what God does, what God offers us, and how God desires to change us. Our scars tell important stories to the one true God. Amen.

Holy Cow, Batman! We are Wholly Known!

Psalm 139:1-18; John 1:43-51

When I was in seminary, right before my final year, I took a summer course called an adventure in wilderness and spirituality. I think I've mentioned this class once before, but I wanted to share a little bit more about my experience. It was a two-week experience and we left Austin, Texas in a van and the professor taped over the clock in the van. We couldn't bring any watches, cellphones, or any type of electronic equipment. He kind of isolated us from knowing the time of day, the goings on in the world, and he kept us from communicating outside of those who were in this van. We took that van and made our way up to Colorado.

Our first week was spent really being challenged. We did low ropes and high ropes courses. How many of you know what those are? They are all about team building. They are low ropes or low activities, that as a team, you have to problem solve and get to the other side. High ropes are generally the same kind of thing where you're up high and sometimes it's an individual thing and sometimes it's a group thing. These courses are all about challenging yourself and reaching beyond yourself.

I can tell you that it was incredibly stressful. I ended up falling off the top rope on one of the high rope courses. I sobbed like a baby because I let my partner down and I was the only one of my fellow students that fell off the rope. Day in and day out, I was faced with my weaknesses and challenges. I was pushed to move beyond and take another step even though I was struggling. Then we spent a week hiking up the mountains in Colorado. We packed up tents, clothing, cooking equipment, and toiletries. My backpack was about thirty-eight pounds and every single day, we were hit with either rain or hail. It was a matter of just getting one foot in front of the other. It didn't matter how tired we were; no man or woman left behind. The final capstone of this adventure was that we were going to spend two nights by ourselves. The professor and our guides took our group out and gave us a section of the meadow and the forest that was ours.

They said, "you can go from here to here and that is your section," and so on. You could come out onto the meadow and get water, but you were not to speak to anyone. You had your journal, your pen, your food, your iodine tablets for your water, your sleeping bag, and your plastic tarp. That first night that we were out, it rained, and we had to figure out a way to take that tarp and protect our sleeping bags and try to stay dry. It was completely horrifying! That next day, everybody hauled their sleeping bags out to the meadow to dry them in the sun.

You couldn't talk to anyone, but you could write in your journal. I recognized that as I was journaling, something was happening internally to me. Something unpleasant was happening internally. The storm clouds started to come back in and we all hauled our sleeping bags back under our tarps. I remember as I got things ready, I looked out over the edge and there was this double rainbow. It was the most vibrant, fluorescent, beautiful double rainbow that I've ever seen but do you think I saw it as that? No, I didn't and what Scripture comes to mind? The story of Noah and the covenant that God makes. My thought was, ha, right God! I didn't have a good attitude about it. The day went on and I continued journaling. I recognized that I was having an internal freak out and I journaled this.

The panic kept rising in me as the day went on. I completely lost it folks! I completely lost it! I'm sobbing in the meadow and I don't know where to go! I decide to go, and I head up and my neighbor asks me if I'm alright even though she isn't supposed to speak to me. I'm bawling and saying that "no, I'm not okay!" I was howling so loud that I sounded like a wounded animal. The professor and the guides came down from the base camp and they found me and tried to calm me down as I was sobbing. They asked me what was wrong, and I just kept saying, "I don't know, I don't know!"

It was absolutely whacked out! I finally calmed down after several hours and they asked me if I wanted to spend the second night out by myself. I said, "no, I don't want to go," and so they walked me down to my camp, helped me get my stuff, and walk it to base camp. It was so embarrassing, and I had no idea what it was about. It wasn't until October of that year, that I realized what it was about. I was sitting in a theology class and the professor happened to be the wife of the professor that took us out into the wilderness. She was talking about Tillich and the Ground of all Being.

As she was talking, I finally realized what had happened in the wilderness in August. I had this panic attack and it was the only panic attack that I've ever had in my life. I finally realized what had happened. I spent day after day being faced with my weaknesses being faced with what I'm strong in and what I'm not strong in. I realized that each day, God was coming closer and closer to me. God was getting so close that I felt like God was about to overtake me. That my being, my ego, was no longer going to be me and God was overtaking me. I freaked out and I ran! Many of us read Psalm 139 and we see it as consolation and comfort.

I can guarantee you that Psalm 139 brought me to tears when I realized what happened to me in that moment in October. Although it's a psalm of consolation, it's also a psalm of recognizing that God knows us so deeply, God is coming toward us, God is consuming us. It is scary as crap, people! Pardon my French, but seriously, think about it! You can't hide from God! God is everywhere! You can't go underground. You can't go to the skies and you can't remove yourself from the spirit of God. God is there! Holy cow Batman, we are completely known, and it frightens me at times to recognize that

God sees that icky underbelly that he sees and knows. God knows all of our failings, all of our shortcomings, all the ways that we fall short. God is there in every single moment even if we don't know it. I want you to take just a moment to think about the one thing that you wish God didn't know about you. Can you think of one thing? Holy cow Batman, you are wholly known! Despite our underbellies, you and I are still loved and called by God to be children of God.

Here we are with the Gospel of John and the calling of Nathaniel. Nathaniel has an aha moment of what is going on. Phillip says to Nathaniel, "come and see, we have found the messiah, Joseph's son out of Nazareth!" I love Nathaniel's response; "can anything good come out of Nazareth?" Can anything good come out of the Republican party? Can anything good come out of the Democratic party? Can anything good come out of Afghanistan? Can anything good come out of families from the east side of Troost? Can anything good come out of Nazareth? Many of the people in this city probably would say, "can anything good come out of the church?" Nathaniel asks a pretty good question but his question kind of shows his underbelly. He's a little judgmental, don't you think? Can anything good come out of Nazareth? Nathaniel decides to go see for himself despite his question and Jesus makes a proclamation about him.

We hear words of affirmation but there's also an interesting thing. When Nathaniel asks how do you know this? Jesus says, "I saw you under the fig tree before Phillip even called you." The fig tree was thought of as an image of safety and security and yet he still decided to come out from under the fig tree to go see Jesus. Jesus says, "despite the fact that you're a judgmental Jewish man, I still see good in you." Jesus saw Nathaniel before Nathaniel ever saw Jesus. He knew Nathaniel and could speak Psalm 139 in that moment. You are wholly known, Nathaniel. Nathaniel's response is, "this is the son of God, the king of Israel, the one to be with!" He says, "holy cow Batman, I am wholly known." Brothers and sisters, this is our season after Epiphany. Epiphany being this season where we celebrate that God in Christ is God! This God completely, wholly knows who we are and calls us to follow even still. It's scary stuff, don't you think, to be completely and wholly known by God? Is anyone else scared or am I the only one? Yet, we are called to follow, to disciple, to come out from under our fig trees, to share that God knows us completely and loves us no matter what. That to me, is empowering news and it means that despite the things that God calls us to, you and I are wholly known. We come to this table to celebrate, that no matter our underbellies, God still loves us so much and would do anything for the folks such as us. Praise be to God. Amen.

It Started with a Fight
Mark 1:21-28

Have any of you at some point in your life, felt like you were an outsider? I certainly have, and I think most of us at some point in time in our lives, have felt like we didn't belong, didn't connect, or that people were keeping us to the fringes.

I had one of those periods of time in my life. I had multiple periods, but this is the one that I'm thinking of right now. I grew up in Kansas City and what I'm about to say is related to a time when I was in high school. I know I have high school connections in the area and I don't want any of them to be offended if they happen to hear this. I went through this period in high school where I was on the outside.

I wasn't part of the cool group of kids. I have my pom-poms here and I'm showing these to you because I was on the pom-pom squad, not the cheerleading squad but the pom-pom squad. We did dance routines and I still have my pom-poms! The pom-pom squad was for the popular girls and I wasn't one of them. I was kind of a dorky girl and had a strange sense of humor. I didn't wear all the cool clothes and my mom liked for us to shop at garage sales quite honestly. That was my life and the funny thing is that I auditioned for the pom-pom squad and I hated being on the pom-pom squad to some degree because I didn't fit in. Many of the girls on the pom-pom squad didn't really want me on the squad either because I was different. I was good enough to make it in my senior year, and I only needed one science class to graduate.

I could have been part of the work study program, but I wasn't because if I chose that, I couldn't have been on the pom-pom squad. Some might ask why in the world would you want to be on the pom-pom squad if you were unhappy with the group of girls? Let me tell you, it's not a great reason and I'm not proud of it now. I really wanted to be on the pom-pom squad because I wanted to be a thorn in those girls' sides! Everybody been there at one time or another? It made me think of this time when I was reading this Scripture. I wanted to place a movie, a cultural piece, during this conversation to kind of frame this Gospel of Mark.

How many of you have seen *The Breakfast Club*? The movie from the 1980's where all of these high school kids end up in detention at the same time for one reason or another. It's a classic film in my opinion because it gets at the angst of high school and the personalities involved. We all had to have known somebody like each of those characters in that movie. Here they were, a mixed pot of teenagers, all with their own issues to be in detention but very much at odds with each other at the beginning of the movie. It's a great movie about the issues that kids and adults deal with but it's also a great theological picture of what can happen when we start revealing our vulnerabilities.

Now, we jump back to the Gospel of Mark. The writer of the Gospel of Mark had a message that he was trying to communicate to the people of faith then and now. He didn't just string a bunch of ideas together, but he had an intention and he was very methodical about the stories that he shared and why he shared them. The writer in this story begins very quickly. The Gospel writer is all about action and it's always active. Right before this passage, Jesus has been baptized and he is tempted by Satan. He then calls his first group of disciples and then we hear this first healing story in the Gospel of Mark.

This story occurs in Capernaum in a synagogue, not in Jerusalem. One of things that we hear in this passage is that the people were odd by the teaching that Jesus was doing. We don't know what the teachings were, but we know they were odd because Jesus was teaching with authority, not like the scribes. This gives us a hint of what Mark wants us to know. Mark wants us to know that Jesus is doing his first miracle on the fringes in Capernaum and that the people were amazed by the authority of his teachings, which was unlike the scribes.

This is important because the scribes were the ones who understood the Torah and they had the knowledge to interpret the Torah for the people. They were about tradition, the purity laws, and remaining steadfast. That's not what Jesus did. Jesus taught not from tradition, not from the purity laws, but Jesus taught with authority. Jesus was doing a new thing! Jesus was proclaiming the Word of God and that if you get stuck by what the scribes say, it's difficult to hear the new message of the kingdom of God. This is where we get information about what that kingdom of God was all about.

The Gospel of Mark talked about what happened in the synagogue that day! Jesus performed a healing, not a cure, and it was a proclamation of what God's kingdom was about. An evil spirit who was inside a man who was able to notice who Jesus was and Jesus said, "be quiet, come out of him." Mark wants us to know that this kingdom of God that Jesus is proclaiming in God's name is a kingdom that is for everybody. It's for those who are on the outskirts, those who aren't part of the in-crowd, those who don't have it all figured out. The kingdom of God is for you and for them! It is a kingdom that is about restoration of a person and reconciliation of a community.

This person who had an evil spirit in him was about the things that could motivate the in-crowd to keep you out of the kingdom and out of the community. Jesus is about bringing healing, a wholeness, and a reconciliation into the community. The thing is that the new teaching that Jesus brings to the status quo freaks the scribes and the Pharisees out! It gets at their power and authority and who likes to give up power? Any of you? Our humanity tends to be such that we aren't easily swayed to let go of our power and authority and to let God have the power.

Mark's Gospel and the healing stories that he weaves together show us that bringing the outsider into the community is one of the things that gets Jesus killed! His authority, his power, and his message about the kingdom of God freaks those people who have authority and power in this world. Jesus says, "God's kingdom is about freedom but in freedom, we have to lose ourselves." You understand that?

It's a challenge and it's difficult for us to really live into that. I wish I would've come up with my sermon title a little later in the week but my sermon title, It Begins with a Fight is true because Mark's Gospel basically begins with a fight. Jesus faces the confrontation of the evil spirit saying, "who the heck do you think you are trying to destroy us?"

I kind of like the sermon title, *The Breakfast Club*. If you all know the movie, some of the characters are part of the in-crowd and some are part of the out-crowd, and yet here they are face to face on a Saturday dealing with detention. They kind of bond because they have a common enemy, but they also reveal their vulnerabilities to each other. They work through the day and by the end of the day, this group of oddballs who shouldn't be a community, become a community of wholeness by being honest with each other.

I wonder if we could figure out a way to be *The Breakfast Club* in this time, this place? Jesus's authority, his proclamation of what the kingdom of God is to be, is still what we are called to live out and be today. For us to be *The Breakfast Club*, we must be willing to reveal our messiness and invite others into it, including the outsiders. They are the ones that we are called to connect with today. I believe as we venture into 2018, we can indeed be *The Breakfast Club*. I believe that we can be willing to have the strength and courage to engage in the same kind of confrontation because that is the kingdom we are called to live in, proclaim and invite. I believe we can be the thorn in the side to those who say it's not possible. May God inspire us, build us up, strengthen us, and encourage us to be that *Breakfast Club*. Amen.

Faith Is Not a Spectator Sport
Luke 1:26-38; 11:20-28

Well, happy Valentine's Day! I'm assuming at this point all of you have purchased your cards for your loved ones and chocolates for your sweetie pie and it's all good. This Valentine's Day, as I was thinking about this Scripture and this celebration of Transfiguration, I thought how in the world can we be speaking of Valentine's Day on this day? This day, we recognize Jesus Christ being transformed in front of his disciples. There is a sort of an understanding of Valentine's Day in the love of God being transformed. I think we need to build on that and flush that out a little bit. This day is kind of the end of the Epiphany season.

The Epiphany that we celebrated at the beginning of the year and this is the day, Epiphany, that we celebrate that all nations recognize that Jesus Christ was the Savior. That Jesus Christ was the one who God sent to bring liberation. That Epiphany is what it is all about; that this human being, Jesus Christ, has come to save and nations recognize that! Today, Transfiguration is another recognition of this same man but slightly different in that it isn't that we recognize the fact that Jesus is fully human. Today, this Transfiguration Sunday, we recognize that Jesus Christ is fully divine, showing God's glory and God's power were in the importance of recognizing him as fully human, fully divine, all embodied in Jesus Christ!

This recognition of Jesus's glory, God's glory, being revealed on this day is an important piece and helps us as we approach the Lenten season to think about all these pieces of who Jesus Christ is! Now, I read this morning from the NLV, or New Living Translation. It's different than the pew Bibles that you all have. The reason why I chose this Scripture work, this translation, was because they translate one of the Greek words in a way that I think is important for our understanding today. So often, you'll find in the NLV, that the word generally gets translated as a departure that Moses and Elijah were talking about.

Jesus's departure can also be translated as death or exodus and the NLV uses the word and it is profound because it conjures up all kinds of imagery, not only for the disciples but for us sitting here. When they heard Jesus talking with Moses and Elijah about his exodus that would be fulfilled in Jerusalem, they conjure up the story of Israel, the act of God, the faithfulness of God, and how God is the one who delivers, who redeems, who saves, and who brings people into their own land.

This is being closely tied by Luke; that Jesus's crucifixion, his death on the cross, is the fulfillment of God's exodus moment. The fulfillment of salvation and liberation that is found in this human where God's divinity is found. Micah even addresses that in this passage. He addresses the whole exodus moment. He lifts the people of Israel to remember that God is faithful and to also remind the people and us that what's happening to them, the darkness that they find themselves in, the struggle that they are living out, are because of the path they chose. God is reminding them in Micah, that they chose a path that separated them from the Lord. They're living their lives in a way that God had not intended. He says, "even though you go through the process of religious festivals and your sacrifices and all of these things that look pretty good, they don't matter."

God says through Micah, "I have shown you, I have told you what is good in our relationship." God says, "it is founded in and grounded on acting justly, to love mercy, and to walk humbly with your God." Now those three things seem simple on the surface. We can do that and that's not a problem. It's very hard for us to live into our relationship that God has invited us into that expects us to act justly, to love mercy, and walk humbly because we continue to be stuck.

We continue to be stuck in the prisons of our own making. How many of you have seen the movie *Groundhog Day*? You know the movie, right? The weather man who thinks he is God's gift to everything and he lives his life pretty much however he wants to, thinking of only himself. He has been called to go see Punxsutawney Phil to report on whether or not the groundhog sees his shadow. He goes to sleep, he wakes up, and he discovers that he's living the same day repeatedly. He finds himself, day after day, waking up and going through the same events. He's trapped in a prison of his own making. Now, he becomes so deep into his despair because there doesn't seem to be a way out of his trap, his prison. He finally decides that he's going to find a way to kill himself, right? He doesn't go through with it though and every morning, he wakes up and relives the day all over.

I think that this is a lot like the way we live our lives of faith; trapped in the prisons of our own making. Whether it is anger that we find in us or we may not even be aware of what causes us to live our lives in a prison. It's not pretty. Perhaps, it is fear that keeps you locked up or maybe it is resentment or your own pride that keeps you from experiencing the glory of God in Jesus Christ! The problem is because we keep in this pattern, we keep living out of our fear and anger.

We're like the man in *Groundhog Day*, living every day over and over, and we don't experience the kingdom of God. One of the things that happens to this character in *Groundhog Day* is profound. He figures, I'm stuck, it doesn't matter what I do so I'm going to take advantage of my time. He learned to play the piano and he starts saving kids falling from trees. He starts living like Micah reminds us to do; to act justly, to love mercy, and to walk humbly. Once he finally has a hold of that, he is released from his prison and he can begin to move into the present and into the future. I think it is hard for us and as we sit here, we admit to ourselves the darkness, the pit of despair that we sit in. I think that it becomes a challenge to be able to understand what it means that in Christ, God's glory, God's exodus, God's salvation, is ours to have hold of. We are a lot like Peter. We get stuck in routine and ritual.

 Peter sees the glory of God and he gets all excited and afraid. He hears them talk about the exodus and he says, "I know what we need to do. We need to build three booths" because all this exodus imagery pops up, right? Part of the exodus celebration is that they would stay in booths because that was part of the exodus life. They were on the move in the wilderness and so they would build booths. They would stay in booths and so this Succoth was in his mind. He fell into the trap and I think we can all sometimes fall into that same trap.

We can easily get stuck in ritual or the same thing. We think that even if we come to church and do our committee meetings, that we pat ourselves on the back and say we've got this religious thing down. Like Peter, we miss the whole event of the Transfiguration, and we miss the glory of God. The next thing we hear about in Luke is that they come down from the mountain and there's this exorcism that happens. Now, there are many people who think this story of the exorcism of this little boy is not really part of the Transfiguration, but I would beg to differ.

I would beg to differ because if this about the exodus, the liberation, and the salvation that comes, and we will see the fulfillment in Jerusalem, then his story is paramount to understanding God's glory and God's desire for us. You see, at the time, they understood evil spirits dwelling within people as the aspect of chaos being present. Chaos that divides us from God and that gets in the way of God's kingdom being fulfilled.

The exorcism of that chaos was so important for the people to understand what Jesus's purpose was, and to tear away the chaos and to break it down so that we could be back in front of God. Jesus's exodus, his crucifixion, this love that is being transformed by a cross is about the healing and the wholeness that is offered to us. Jesus heals the boy, sends chaos away, and then he does something so important. He takes the boy after he's been healed, and he gives the boy back to his father.

You see, Jesus wants us to embrace the healing and the wholeness that he offers in his life on the cross. He heals us and then he offers us back to God, our Father. Now, I imagine that many of you are like me, and we think about the things that we do when we think that we have done what we need to do with our faith. Faith is not a spectator sport. What we believe doesn't give us the right to just sit in our pews, go through the motions, and think we've got it covered!

Christ calls us out of the stands and onto the field to become active players in the game! Christ calls us to act justly, to love mercy, and to walk humbly. How many of you can honestly say that you have had an experience with the holy Jesus Christ? How many of you can say that you have embraced that beauty and that power and in doing so, you have been changed? Your faith is not a spectator sport, but your faith is actively engaged in the wholeness God gives us. I've had those moments, but I am still waiting for the courage to get a new perspective on Jesus, and to see what the Transfiguration really is and how I can be changed. God's love is transformed on the cross. God's love calls us from our seats to be a part of the game. Are you all willing to join the game? Are you all ready to play? That is the question for us today. Are we going to be in the game? Happy Valentine's Day. Amen.

Just a Little Off the Top, Please
John 15:5-8

For as long as I can remember, the Gospel of John has really been my favorite Gospel. Its rich complexities, analogies, and symbolic language have always thrilled me. I must tell you that as I have been wrestling with the Scriptures this last week, I've had a difficult time embracing the Gospel of John. There is so much that goes on in this one passage that it's hard to wrap my brain around one idea that I could really share with you.

Part of the problem is that this passage is so familiar to us. How many of us have heard this passage and heard sermons given time after time? What is it that I could say that would be new and different and something that we haven't thought about? That was a struggle for me. Then, I really came to terms with the fact that maybe this time around, it isn't about finding something that we haven't heard but to speak what we've already heard to remind us of the truth of God. Maybe even more so in this time, we need to remember to be reminded.

As I wrestled with this passage, and really worked to grab a hold of some sort of meaning, there were words that just popped out at me. They were action words such as abide or remain, bearing fruit, and pruning. One of the things that struck me was that all of these words in the context of this passage have at the center of them, a small portion of fear. This is because each of them implicates or leads to something that requires accountability, vulnerability, risks, and something that calls us to account.

Those words, for me, kind of cause a little fear. I find the words abide in me or remain in me to be a very big struggle. Maybe for many of you, the idea of trying to live out, to understand, and to have a grasp of what it means to abide in Christ, is a struggle. I can honestly say that I know that I have fallen short of praying unceasingly. I know that I have been guilty of living into some of the sinful natures, bearing grudges, and listening to the other voices that we lifted in our prayer of confession that lead me, lead us away from remaining steadfast in Christ.

What does it mean to remain, to abide in Christ? Perhaps for me, the thing that causes even more fear and causes me to realize how much more I'm called to risk, is not necessarily just abiding in Christ but it's the other piece that Jesus lifts up. He says, "abide in me as I abide in you." That is a little scary to me because if I actually let Jesus abide in me, take root in my soul and spirit, that means I have to get out of the way.

Is that as scary for you as it is for me? Allowing Christ to actually remain in means being vulnerable, taking risks, and means I have to trust what that relationship is all about. It's very interesting to me, as we hear this passage in the Gospel of John, it starts with this imagery of God the Father being the vine dresser and Jesus being the vine. The realization that as this goes on, Jesus says, "it first starts with him." He says, "God is the vine dresser, I am the vine and what God does is God looks at me." Jesus says, "God looks at me and the branches that are in me and looks at what is not producing fruit and he cuts those branches off me." Jesus goes on to say that, "God looks at me and sees what branches are bearing fruit and prunes them so that they can produce even more fruit." He says, "it starts with me," and then he calls us to recognize our interrelationship with him by being the branches that are in him, realizing that we do not stand there alone but we are then part of the vine. If we abide in him and allow him to abide in us, we possibly have a little more focus.

There's this paradoxical sort of imagery that plays out with Isaiah and this Gospel of John passage. Is it about taking hold and doing the work to make sure that the fruit is being produced or is it about allowing God to make sure that the fruit is being produced? For many of us, we think that how we show our fruit is by all of the things we do, the acts we take, and the way we live our lives. If we are producing fruit, then we're good to go. Yet, our theology tells us that we can't do anything! We can't work our way into the kingdom and we can't do enough things to earn salvation to actually be a part of the vine! This creates tension.

It is God who nurtures us, who fertilizes us, who prunes us, who takes good care of us. He is the wonderful caretaker of us. Yet, there is this call of accountability, that if we trust in that caretaker's love for us, we will be inclined and motivated to be productive in our lives. How we bear our fruit ties us back to making sure that Christ is actually abiding in us because we can't bear fruit on our own.

I can tell you that many of us, including myself, are well-intentioned about all the things we do, all the deeds we live out, all for the good of the church. Yet, if we're honest and looked at them, we might discover that we haven't been abiding in Christ and Christ hasn't been abiding in us. We have to look honestly at what we're doing. The other action word, pruning, is also, very, very scary for me. How about you? For me, I want to think that I'd be okay with God taking a pair of pruning shears to me but when it gets down to the brass knuckle, I'd tell God what needs to be pruned. I want to say, "just take a little bit off the top, please."

I figure I'm in control, but I've missed the boat when it comes to abiding in, trusting in, and allowing the pruning to take place. The pruning is not a bad thing. It is about taking the shears to that which is already producing good fruit so that it can be even more productive. Again, that takes a lot of trust in the one who's got a hold of the pruning shears. The interesting thing about this story is that Jesus puts before us the interesting way that many of us have gone down the path. I have heard it. We're okay with the whole I am the vine, you are the branches, abide in me, I abide in you. We're even okay with pruning and making what is fruitful even more fruitful. We get buggy eyed when we get to the part that we hear when something isn't producing, it withers and dies, and it will be thrown into the fire and burned away.

Often, how we read that is that God is that mean and judgmental God, right? How could he throw us into the fire if we're not on task? I think both Isaiah and John challenge that notion because the truth is that it's not written anywhere in the text. You see, the truth that John is trying to get at is that if we ourselves aren't available to allow God to prune us and to shave off what we don't need, we've made the decision to disconnect ourselves. We then are responsible for the withering, dying, and being thrown into the fire. Jesus in the Gospel of John is trying to encourage us to understand the consequences of our stubbornness, of our resistance when we walk that path.

That's when we find ourselves on the path away from the goodness of God. Being pruned is not an easy thing. It can be quite painful because it means letting go of the superficial pieces in our lives. Each of our lists of things that need to be let go of or pruned would be different, but it remains that we are all in that place. What are the things in your life that need to be pruned? What has God been pruning lately? The thing that is very dangerous is to just think that this Scripture is about us as individuals and what do I need to do as an individual to make myself available for God to prune? If I stay in that place, I miss an important piece of what Jesus wants me, wants us, to realize.

Jesus wants us to realize that this is about the relationship in relating with the vine, relating with Christ, and in relating with the Father! You see, Jesus pulls on a symbolic image that is so powerful in the mind of the Jews. He lifts up the image of the vineyard and for the Jews, the vineyard is the image of the community of the people of Israel, the people of God. Jesus is very intentional to say, "you are all a part of this vine and you are all the people of God." This is something that we need to remember as the body of Christ.

Where do we as the body of Christ, as a community of faith, need to make ourselves available to God, trusting that God loves us, and that God knows what is best for us as a community of faith? What are the branches that really aren't producing fruit anymore and need to be cut off? Do we have the courage to be honest with ourselves? When we look at the things that are producing fruit in this place and I can tell you that we are, are we satisfied with what fruit is being produced in us? Are we willing to allow God to prune us so that we can be even more fruitful? We are the body of Christ and if we remain in him and he remains in us, we can trust the shape, and the pruning that God does with us. Are you ready to be pruned? Are we courageous enough to be pruned? God desires for us to be fruitful vines, fruitful branches. Will we be? My hope is that we together as a community will find the strength and courage to be that what God calls us to be, what God calls us to do. I pray that what we will see in the end is the beautiful vision that God sees of us. The fruitful vine of Christ our Lord. How will the future look? The future is ours. Amen.

The Pot Stirrer
Acts 2:1-21

I want you to think back over the generations of your life, the decades of your life. I want you to recall one big moment, a watershed moment, that you knew was going to change the course of this nation, of your life, of what was going on in this world. What would be that watershed moment for you? Perhaps, it was the Vietnam War or perhaps it was the assassination of JFK.

Maybe for those of you from my generation, the watershed moment was the tearing down of the Berlin Wall. Maybe that watershed moment for those of you that are younger, was 9/11. We all can think of that big moment when we knew things would never be the same. The church has a major watershed moment. Even beyond the birth, life, death, and resurrection of Jesus Christ, the big watershed moment for the church is today, it's Pentecost. The day when the Holy Spirit is given to us and pushes us out into the world. This is the watershed moment for us today and nothing will be the same.

This day of Pentecost is an astounding day! It was the day that Jesus told the disciples to wait for it because when it comes, you will be given great power. When the Holy Spirit came, and it did, it brought great power! When we hear this description in Acts, the giving of the Holy Spirit, it's one of a violent wind of fire that is known for its destructive powers.

Another image for the Holy Spirit is great waters because it's chaotic and has great power. These images show us that God is up to something huge on this day. Pentecost is really an important day, but it isn't just about the Holy Spirit coming. It's fifty days after the Passover. Remember they are Jews celebrating a special day, Pentecost. This wasn't just for Christians; it was for the Jews as well. Fifty days after the Passover, they were celebrating this thing that

God does. God is the one who gives. In response and gratitude to what God does, this Pentecost season was about giving back the first fruits. It is about recognizing who God is, what God does for us, and who we are as God's people. There they were, the disciples of Jesus Christ, holding up and waiting for something to happen. Then it did. The Holy Spirit descended on them, and in the process, they were overtaken and speaking these languages even though they were all Galilean.

In that room, all of the power and chaos sparked the interest of the Jews who were there for this Pentecost. It caused them to say, "what in the world is going on?" and they came to discover what was happening. They heard this good news in their own language. Isn't it amazing? They are hearing something about what God does. God forgives, and he gives second chances, and invites them into the work that God does. God loves, redeems, and he saves, and they are hearing this. I think the Holy Spirit gets shafted in the Presbyterian Church. As Presbyterians, we're lovingly known to others as the "frozen chosen."

You giggle because you know it's true. Presbyterians; we're good with God the Father, we're good with Jesus Christ the Son, but we're not exactly comfortable with the Holy Spirit. With the Holy Spirit comes unpredictability, and it's something we can't control. We can't shape it or put it in a box because as Presbyterians, we like to do things decently and in order. We like to shy away from this Holy Spirit thing. Saints, even as Presbyterians, we now in this day need to recognize the power of the Holy Spirit! You see, this power of the Holy Spirit is now today!

We need to remember and embrace and let the power of the Holy Spirit fill us! The work that is out there for us to do is serious. We've got Israelites and Palestinians killing each other and it is serious. We've got school shootings and it is serious. There is pain and hurt and it is deep. We need the Holy Spirit and we need this watershed moment, especially now. We need to allow the Holy Spirit to do what it does. You see, the Holy Spirit, is a pot stirrer. It comes along, and it stirs the pot, agitates the waters, fans the flames. It really pushes us, especially as good Presbyterians, out of our comfort zone.

It pushes us to move beyond the boundaries of what we would like to stay in. Now in this church, many of you know, we're having to face the pot stirrer because we are in the midst of doing something different. It's a perfect story for us today. If we're going to live into the Holy Spirit and let the pot stirrer stir our pot as people of faith, we have to let the Holy Spirit speak through us to others. You see, if we really embrace this Holy Spirit, we have to allow God to use us and speak a language to others, so they can hear the Word of God for them. Do you understand what I'm saying? We cannot be comfortable anymore. I have a friend and she told me a story.

A pastor in a church wanted to start figuring out a way to communicate the Gospel to youth. They started playing around with worship, music, hands-on activities, etc. A member of the church came up to my friend and said, "when you put screens in the sanctuary, I'm out of here!" "I'm out of here if you try to push me out of my comfort zone." Many of us are comfortable in how we think the Holy Spirit speaks to us.

We've forgotten how important it is that the Holy Spirit speaks not just to us but how the Holy Spirit speaks to others through us. Can we allow the Holy Spirit to stir the pot in our lives, to confront the disappointments we see in ourselves and in the world? Can we allow the Holy Spirit to stir our pot as individuals and as a community of faith? Are we going to remain like that woman who said, "once those video screens show up in my sanctuary, I'm out of here?" Today is our watershed moment to have the Holy Spirit to transform us and to have the community ask are they drunk?

On the cover of your bulletin, there's a quote from Pastor Steven Furdeck, a pastor in North Carolina. Are you reading it? "If the size of your vision for your life isn't intimidating to you, there's a good chance it's insulting to God." It's true not just for us as individuals but for us as the body of Christ. If we're afraid for the Holy Spirit to create chaos in us, through us, and around us, then perhaps our vision is insulting to God.

I pray that this indeed can be really, deeply, truly a watershed moment for us. That the Holy Spirit transforms us and that we as individuals and as the body of Christ will never be the same because the Holy Spirit infuses us and will do mind boggling, chaotic, fire breathing, flooding things in this world! May the Holy Spirit fill us, stir within us, and stir us in this world. Can I get an Amen? Amen.

We've Got a Long Way to Go and a Short Time to Get There
Genesis 12:1-9; Mark 2: 1-12

The path of least resistance; it's the path that we can choose to take that's easier, right? It's easier to flip through a magazine than to read your Bible. It might be easier to play and waste time on the computer than to play with your children. It might be easier to post on social media, some sort of comment on Facebook or Twitter, than to actually engage in conversation with an acquaintance or even quite honestly family and friends.

The path of least resistance is when we make choices that seem to be less painful and often more pleasant. There's a story that I heard about a pastor. I don't know if it's true or not but it's a fun story about a pastor who had seen a neighborhood cat in a tree. The cat had climbed the tree and could not make its way down. Have you all heard this story before? The cat is in this tree and the pastor is trying to coax the cat with tuna because he's afraid the tree isn't going to hold him, so he can't climb the tree to get the cat. He decided that he's going to take a rope and tie it to one of the tree limbs and tie it to the back of his car. He's going to slowly move the car forward so the tree will slowly come down.

Are you with me so far? He pulls that tree down, and he feels like it's not down far enough, so he moves forward just a little bit. Well, the rope breaks and the cat goes flying through the air. He searches all over the neighborhood for this cat. He goes door to door looking for this cat with no luck. He finally says to himself that he doesn't even want to think about what happened to that cat. Well, a couple of days later, the pastor is in the grocery store and one of his parishioners is there buying cat food. He knows this parishioner hates cats and so he asks her why are you buying cat food? She says, "well funny story." "My daughter has been begging and begging for a cat." She tells her daughter to pray to God for a cat and if God delivers a cat to you, you can have the cat. She says, "you wouldn't believe it, but my daughter went outside, and she got on her knees and prayed to God for a cat and out of the air, a cat came flying into her arms."

Well, our life as people of faith is kind of like that cat being flung from the tree. It's not necessarily the easiest way to remove oneself from a tree but we have a tendency to be stuck in a tree sometimes as people of faith God has to boomerang the tree and throw us out across the sky to get us to where God needs us. That's a lot like our Scriptures today. I love these Scriptures from Genesis and Mark. Imagine if you were Abram, he later is known as Abraham, but in this story he's Abram. Abram is comfortable with the land and he's been there for years with his family.

Imagine that your family lives around you and you have the security of knowing how to make a living. Even though you're seventy-five years old, you feel like life is good and how it should be. Then God shows up and God says to you as Abram, "I want you to go to a land where I will show you." God speaks ambiguous blessings but despite that, God calls you to go immediately. How would you respond? Would you go? I think I'd be like, "say what?" Here is the case of the paralytic in the Gospel of Mark.

You've been outcast by society and your family doesn't really embrace you because you are the symbol of quite possibly sins of the father. That is how they understood illness at that time. It was believed that illness, disease, was a sign that someone, either in your family or you, had sinned. The community didn't embrace you, but despite all of that, you made your way. You had someone carry the mat for you. You had the security of knowing what your life was about. You could lay on your mat and somehow people felt pity and provided for you by throwing coins at you. Then one day, four friends come along and pick you up and carry you. They don't ask you if you're interested in being healed. They pick you up, march you through a crowd of people, hoist you up on a ceiling, dig through the roof and lower you down on a mat in front of Jesus. Jesus says, "your sins are forgiven." He says to you, "get up, take your mat, and walk out." What would you say as a paralytic? Again, I might say, "say what?"

The life you've known has been changed by being healed. Do you want to go out into the world and have to now work when you're used to people giving you stuff? Do you want to deal with reconciling with your family and friends? It's not an easy task to be transformed and healed. I think that there is a hint of the humanity in Abram and what has happened in the Gospel passage to speak to our human tendency to take the path of least resistance. God doesn't allow us to get away with that. God challenges us to take the path of resistance, the path that is challenging, difficult, the path that calls us take risks and to make sacrifices to this life God calls us to. It is a life of transformation but it's not without fear and trepidation. Here at South-Broadland, let me be frank with you, we have a very sparse group of people sitting here this Sunday. You all have called me to be your pastor.

The Heartland Presbytery really believes that South-Broadland has one year left to survive financially before the doors will have to be closed. The PNC and the Session think that there might be two years. We have two years to experience the possibility of being flung from that tree and to land somewhere else. The reality is that we see three options. We can continue to do this, and we'll have to close the doors in a year if we keep doing the same thing and stay in our comfort zone.

The second option would be finding our new understanding of our identity, transforming, reaching out and inviting, and being Christ's kingdom in the world. It takes actual effort and it means every single one of us are participating. There is another option as well. There's the possibility of selling this building and finding the place that God is calling us to move to into another location. Are you all with me so far? We have the option to choose the path of least resistance and continue to do the same thing. We also have the option of choosing the path of great resistance that might mean selling the building and moving and taking part of that heritage with us but allowing God to transform us! Abram answered God's call and Abram went. I think we may be like Abram. We go but we get ourselves tripped up when we think we know what that land should look like. We find out that this land that God shows us is filled with people, but not just any people, but with Canaanites. I can imagine Abram saying, "did I hear God right?" We trip ourselves up when we think we know what it is, and we have to just go without a lot of reflection. The Scriptures are immediate and say, "go, pick up your mat, and walk." What will we do? Will we choose the path of least resistance? Will we just decide that it's better, easier, and it's more pleasant to go down this path instead of risking, changing, and transforming, which is much more difficult? We do have a long way to go and by Presbyterian standards, we have a short time to get there. My prayer is as we step out of the circle of comfort, as we change things in our worship, as we're challenged to take on a new identity and ministry, that we allow God to shape us, transform us, and show us that land and trust that there will be blessings for us and the people that God takes us to. We've got a long way to and a short time to get there. Are you ready to be flung from the tree? Amen.

E = mc2: Live Life Differently
Leviticus 19:9-18; Matthew 5:38-48

I'm going to be reading from Eugene Peterson's *The Message*. It's not a strict sort of translation. It's more of an interpretation and it's kind of like his approach to translating Scripture with his own sort of agenda. The thing that I like about his interpretation of this reading is that I think it gets a little bit more at the heart of the Greek language. It was written in a way that has a little bit more profound meaning for us. I want you to listen to the Gospel of Matthew and hear what Jesus is saying. This is the Gospel of Matthew, chapter five and if you want to read along, you'll see the differences between what is in your bulletin, the NIV, and this is *The Message*;

> *Here's another old saying that deserves a second look: 'Eye for eye, tooth for tooth.' Is that going to get us anywhere? Here's what I propose: 'Don't hit back at all.' If someone strikes you, stand there and take it. If someone drags you into court and sues for the shirt off your back, giftwrap your best coat and make a present of it. And if someone takes unfair advantage of you, use the occasion to practice the servant life. No more tit-for-tat stuff. Live generously.*

> *You're familiar with the old written law, 'Love your friend,' and its unwritten companion, 'Hate your enemy.' I'm challenging that. I'm telling you to love your enemies. Let them bring out the best in you, not the worst. When someone gives you a hard time, respond with the energies of prayer, for then you are working out of your true selves, your God-created selves. This is what God does. He gives his best— the sun to warm and the rain to nourish—to everyone, regardless: the good and bad, the nice and nasty. If all you do is love the lovable, do you expect a bonus? Anybody can do that. If you simply say hello to those who greet you, do you expect a medal? Any run-of-the-mill sinner does that.*

*In a word, what I'm saying is, Grow up. You're kingdom subjects.
Now live like it. Live out your God-created identity. Live generously
and graciously toward others, the way God lives toward you.*

Love your enemies. Those really are challenging words from our
Lord. Not necessarily just for this time in our world because I think
there has been a nastiness, grittiness, ugliness, brokenness, since the
beginning of time. These are still challenging words, nonetheless, to
love your enemies and pray for them. I wanted to tell you that I
understand the difficult nature of to love your enemy. Some of you
know but most of you don't know, that the last time I served a
church was seven years ago.

Quite honestly, my departure from that church was a really nasty
departure because there were people in that congregation and
leadership that out of politics, out of a meanness, out of their own
agendas, decided that they didn't want me as their associate pastor.
They got rid of me in not a very Christian way. I had to go to the
Associate Executive Presbyter of that Presbytery to help me respond
in a Christ like way to the pain and the hurt that was my life. I will
be honest with you, I really wrestled because in my spirit, I would
visualize less than pleasant things that would happen to those
people. I even thought of ways to facilitate that ugliness, but the
Lord blessed me and helped restrain me from going down that path.

Now, I don't always say that I've come to love them, but I have
gotten much closer as I've moved forward in my life. Love your
enemies. It is a challenging thing for us to do. It seems like it's
magnified in this political arena that we see around us. We are to love
our neighbors as ourselves, not just the people that live next door or
the people that we sit next to in the pews, but the people across the
city and nation that don't necessarily have the same ideals that we
have. Jesus is starting a revolution with these words that it's no more
eye for eye, tooth for tooth because we'd all end up pretty blind if
we followed that.

He challenges people to not respond with violence and to not respond in the way in which the world tends to respond. We see it all around us, don't we? We see people responding to disagreements and hurt and saying and doing things that leave a huge mess! Jesus doesn't call us to be doormats though. The turn the other cheek, give your coat in addition, and go the extra mile are ultimately about subverting the power in way that is God like. We are different people!

We are God's creation and we are to live as though we are! The Leviticus passage is really echoed in this passage from Matthew. It is calling up for memory of the Ten Commandments and the ways that we engage in relationship with others. It's about justice, love, and honoring each other's humanity, even with strangers. It calls us to be holy people because Leviticus is that book that is written for the priestly people. We are priestly people, people! We are to be holy, set apart, and engaging in these kinds of actions like in the Leviticus and Matthew passages.

God through Christ calls us to engage each other with justice, love, peace, and understanding, not with violence, aggression, and anger in our hearts. I have a couple of things to think about. What does it mean to be living justly, lovingly, and engaging our neighbors? In your bulletin, you all have a brochure that has our Lenten worship experience. I hope that you will take time and engage in our Lenten journey. I really encourage you to take an extra brochure and invite others into this revolutionary journey. It's a great time for us to start engaging each other in this walk of faith and revolution to understand what this relationship with Christ is.

The one that goes to the cross for us, that is our Lenten journey! I challenge you to hand one of these to a friend, a neighbor, a co-worker. I don't want to just sit there, and I hope you all don't want to just sit there. Last week, I told you all what the Presbytery said our future was if things did not change. I certainly hope that you all are willing to prove the Presbytery wrong in a Christ like way. We must start thinking about what it means to reach out because that is what we're called to do! We're called to justice and to offer the transforming life that comes with being in a relationship with God. We need to figure out what our niche is, what we're called to. I thought of some awesome ministry ideas. Are you ready? We could be engaged in Kairo's Prison Ministry. Has anybody heard of that? It is an opportunity to offer ministry to those who have been incarcerated or to family members of those who have been incarcerated. It is a way to talk about justice and love and offer that transforming word to people who really need it.

We could do something as simple as offering this place as a cooling house in the summer for people who may not have air conditioning. Why not offer people a place of respite on those hot, summer days? We've got plenty of space, right? What if we did a Vacation Bible School in Tower Park? We could host a job fair for those who are looking for employment. We could also offer GroovaRroo dance classes for mothers and fathers with babies and help them be in step with their families.

What about Pink and Dude Café? It's an after school culinary experience that started in California for middle schoolers. They could learn about nutrition and cooking and it's twice a week. Doesn't that sound exciting? We could partner with the colleges, YMCA, and the Boys and Girls Club to help with this project. What about a community garden? We have a huge piece of land and my husband sent me information about using hay bales for the garden instead of fertilizer and dirt. What a great way to use the land that God has blessed us with and also help families learn about gardening and sustainability?

We could have a children's theater for first through sixth graders over the summer and have a theater camp and performance. We could offer a car clinic once a month for single mothers and widows and help them ensure that their cars are running efficiently. We could teach youth about bicycle maintenance. We could take lunches to firemen and teach English as Second Language (ESL) classes to anyone that may need this service. We need to petition the city for a crosswalk so that the people across the street can come here to worship and learn about God's love.

There are endless opportunities for us to engage and for us to be the people that Jesus calls us to be. $E = mc2$, do you all know that equation?

I'm terrible at math so I defined that as evangelism=mission, community times two to the second power. I found a guy, Joshua Carol, who decided to make this equation make sense in human power. He broke it down in human being into joules of energy. He says, "one Josh is the energy and it equals 7.76x10 to the 18th power." This equals 1,856,459 kilotons of TNT. He goes on, "thus concluding our little mind experiment, we find that just one human being is roughly equal to 1.86 million kilotons worth of energy."

That's a lot! He goes on, "let's put this in perspective just to illuminate the massive amount of power that this equivalence really is." "The bomb that destroyed Nagasaki in Japan during World War II was devastating." "That bomb was approximately 21 kilotons of explosives so that means that one human being has 88,403 times more explosive energy than a bomb that destroyed an entire city." That goes for every human being! We need to start living differently! We need to start this revolution of bringing God's kingdom to people and we have an amazing amount of potential energy.

It means loving our enemies and engaging with love, compassion and mercy. It means being holy people and reaching out and showing the power that this congregation has. If we engage out there, imagine the explosion of positiveness we will have in this world for our Lord and Savior.

Who's ready to be a member of this revolution? Come on! Who's ready? I want you to sit down and brainstorm ideas for ways you can engage in mission and ways we can engage in mission as a community. I've already started a nice list, but we need to come together and show this great power of our church and be that revolution! Let's live life differently! Can I get an Amen? Amen.

Out of the Box and Into the Frying Pan
Exodus 24:9-18; Matthew 17:1-18

Before I start the Word this morning, I want to say to all of you that next week, the first Sunday of Lent, our Scripture is going to lead us into addressing the subject of the killing of the young man in Kansas. You all know the story of whom I'm talking about? The Indian man who was killed? Our passage out of Genesis next week is really going to confront us.

We're going to engage in that subject. I wanted you all to be aware that I am aware of that and we are going to address that but our message for today is a little bit different. Transfiguration is a time for us to really stand in awe of who Jesus Christ is. This moment that he becomes so beautiful, so illuminated and we hear that he is indeed God's son. It is something that brings us to our knees and at the same time, we stand amazed.

We are touched by how God engages us and shows us who he is in Christ. That leads us to think about how many times we might have had those mountain top experiences. Has anybody here had one of those times where you were just so enveloped in what God is doing and what God has shown to you and you've just had a great feeling of waahhaaa? Anybody? Let me see hands. I want to see hands! Anybody? Some of you?

Well, these are amazing experiences, but the funny thing is, we have a tendency to respond to those moments like Peter. Peter is one of the disciples on the mountain with Jesus, and the first thing he wants to do is what? He wants to build a tent, a tabernacle, a place where Jesus, Elijah, and Moses and can camp for the night. Let's just enjoy the moment.

We have a tendency to want to set up camp in those mountain top moments, right? This is the problem. You may have heard that we shouldn't put God in a box. How many of you have heard that little phrase? I think our Scriptures actually challenge us about not just putting God in the box but of being aware of not putting ourselves in the box.

Is there feedback? Is there feedback out there? Can you all hear me if I'm in the box? I heard feedback in the box but maybe that's Jesus again. When we build those tents on those mountain top moments and when we put ourselves in the box, all we can see is the box. We can't see what God is doing. We can't be called to move anywhere because we're stuck in our box. I think that's one of the things in this Scripture that challenges us because Peter wants to build that box and have everyone join him in that box. Jesus calls us out of the box.

He doesn't even allow Peter to get too far along on that thinking. He tells Peter to stand up and don't be afraid and don't stay in the box. I think sometimes as churches, we don't even realize that we're in the box. We want to keep those glory years of how we were as a church up and around us. We want to stay in those glory year boxes and we miss what God is calling us to. Jesus, he calls us to a different place. He says to them as they're heading down the mountain, "listen, I do not want you to tell anybody about this experience until much later."

I think it's a warning because if we keep on talking about the box, about that mountain top experience, we trap ourselves from being engaged in what God calls us to do. God calls us down from the mountain. He calls us out of our boxes and we have to fight to come out of our box. God calls us out of our boxes, out of those mountain top moments and he brings us back down the mountain to do what? The first thing that Jesus does when he comes down the mountain is he heads right into mission, service, healing, and wholeness. He says, "if I am God's son, if I am where God is shining, and it is passed on to all of you, it comes with the responsibility to be in ministry, to be serving, to be launching ourselves into the community to help those who are demon possessed, who are ill, who are broken, who need to be liberated, and to know what it means to have a resurrected life."

Last week, we talked about the possibility of mission, outreach, and I laid before all of you, some ideas. I challenged all of you to think about what mission, what outreach, God might be calling you to be involved in and to bring ideas to this place. How many of you did that? Awesome, I knew I could count on some of you. Now, I'm going to count on all of you because you're going to have an opportunity.

You see, in your bulletin, you have sticky notes. I want you to pull that sticky note out and write down one or two ideas of mission. Frederick Buechner says, "our purpose in life, our vocation, is where our greatest passion intersects with the world's greatest need." In that Venn diagram, in that intersection, where our greatest passion is, and our world's greatest need is, that is where we can find our purpose, our mission.

I want you to take a moment and reflect on what is God calling you, I, and the church to do. As we come down from the mountain, out of our boxes, and into the frying pan of mission, what is God calling us to do? Take a moment, just a moment. Our Lord loves us and trusts us so much with taking his Word out and being that Word in the community.

My hope is that we are ready to come out of our boxes and into that frying pan. Are you ready? Amen, brother! This morning, when we collect our offering, I want you to bring those sticky notes with you and put your sticky note on the outside of the box. We're going to collect those, and as a community, discern where those ideas may lead us from the mountain top and down the mountain into ministry. Amen.

What's in Your Wallet?
Mark 14:1-11

What's in your wallet? If we were to ask you to open up your wallet or your purse, what would we find in there? Will there be a lot of money in there? "Nope!" What about credit cards? How many of you have credit cards? Yep, that's me as well. I have a couple of other bizarre things in my wallet as well. I have my scuba diver certification cards in my wallet. How many of you have those in your wallet?

Well, I think this passage really does beg us to consider what we might have in our wallets. Do you see where I'm going with this? This passage is kind of a unique passage. It's kind of a sandwich passage. It starts off with the Jewish leaders, the religious leaders, trying to find a way that they can take Jesus down, right? That's the first layer of bread. The top layer of bread in this sandwich is it ends with Judas Iscariot deciding that he is indeed going to betray Jesus. He goes to those people and says, "I've got a deal for you," and they love this idea.

They are willing to put a little cash in his wallet to have Jesus betrayed and to give them what they want. We've got people planning nefarious things and in the middle of this sandwich is this story of a woman who comes uninvited to a party and she does something quite shocking. She breaks open an alabaster jar of pure nard and she anoints Jesus. She wasn't invited to this party and there's probably some that would say that the disciples and Simon the Lepper were all men.

Why in the world is this uninvited woman coming here and showing off, right? I want you to take just a moment with this story in mind and try to picture who you are. Who are you if we were to find you in this story? Are you one of the religious leaders or teachers of the law that are trying to trap Jesus? Now, I'm sure some of you would say, "heck no, not me!" Are you the disciples sitting around the table? You've been following Jesus with loyalty and commitment and you're hanging on every word. Are you Simon the Leper and although you've probably been healed by Jesus, you're still known by the title of leper. If you were a leper, you had to go through town with a bell ringing and say, "unclean, unclean!" Are you this unnamed woman bringing a gift and anointing Jesus?

There's another option that we don't want to claim that we are. We don't want to be Judas. We don't want to be the one that is the impetus for Jesus being ratted out. Who are we as a community of faith in this story? I think that we like to think we're the good person in the story but if we look at what was underneath the motivation, we might be able to say there's a hint of the disciples or Judas in us. People who really struggle to have control in their lives want things to work by their own agenda.

If we're honest as individuals and as a community of faith, we have had moments that are motivated just by those things. Here comes this uninvited guest who we would love to say we are. She takes an expensive jar, breaks it open and she anoints Jesus. It really is an irrevocable waste because once she breaks the jar open, there's no turning back. One of the other interesting pieces of this story is this act by this woman is an act of a gift. How many real gifts do we hear about people giving to Jesus in the Gospel reading? Not many, right?

Most of the time, it is Jesus who is giving. He is bringing healing, wholeness, community, inclusion, and equality. He is bringing tons of gifts to the people and very rarely do we hear of someone bringing a gift to Jesus. It begs the question what's in your wallet? What are we really willing to give? Are we willing to give a whole year's wages to our Lord? Are we really wiling to break open that jar of ourselves and pour ourselves out before our Lord? This was kind of a strange turn of events for me. I was not really being one who was inclined to talk about stewardship, but the Lord led me there anyway. I was going to talk about stewardship after Easter, but God said, "no, today we are going to talk about what we are willing to give." How many of you know what tithing is? Ten percent, right? There's some biblical reference to that but I wonder if God is actually more concerned with the ninety percent, the ninety percent that we hold onto.

If we understand that everything that we have is from God and we are stewards, meaning that we have been given the responsibility to manage these things very well, and God says, "you give ten percent back to me." Is that where his concern lies and the other ninety percent, we just do what we want? Is that who God is? No! Since I have been here, almost two months, I've had you all do something that is a really important step in understanding that everything we have belongs to God.

I've been giving you a slip of paper in the bulletin that says God, "this week, I'll give to you." I've said to you, if you don't have any financial gift to give, fill out the piece of paper and put it in the offering plate. Even if you do have a financial gift, go ahead and fill the paper out and turn it in. When we first did this, the responses were lacking something, but I have to tell you that after the first week, these sheets of paper have been profound.

They've really started working toward this understanding of everything that you've been given is a gift from God! These answers are beginning to show that you are developing a sense of depth and I want to encourage all of you to keeping moving forward in that. We do need to talk about the money piece. Some of you may be at a place where you give ten percent and some of you may be somewhere in the middle.

There are also some of you who don't put even a dollar in the plate. I want you take just a moment and think about why you haven't put something in the plate. What is that about? I think God challenges us in just the mere act of putting something in that offering plate if we're giving with the intention of love and thankfulness and being stewards.

Yes, that money helps pay for this building, my salary, and other things but that's the reality of what it means to be the body of Christ. Hopefully, it means that some of that money actually goes to the body of Christ outside. How many of you see yourself in the act of breaking open your heart, a vessel, your wallet and pouring all of its contents before God and that Jesus in seeing what you do is so thankful? I want you to take a piece of this pottery and I want you to carry this with you and I want you to consider your own life of stewardship. I want you to consider what it means for you to be broken, completely poured out to the one who gave everything to us. The disciples' response to this woman was one of jealousy. Their hearts went to a really dark place.

Instead of celebrating and recognizing what this woman was doing, they thought that this woman could have sold that, and they could've given money to the poor and they could've looked good. Let us not be stingy disciples, let us be the overwhelmingly gracious woman who comes and breaks our lives open for the one who has offered us everything in being. This is our Lenten journey. We are headed to the crucifixion of our Lord and Savior. We cannot pretend that it doesn't exist, and we cannot pretend that we are the owners of the stuff we have! I know that we get scared and hold on to security but that keeps us from pouring ourselves out.

Discipleship is about risk, trusting God, and pouring ourselves out completely. If your heart isn't in your wallet, it's empty. So, what is in your wallet? Are we courageous enough to look? Amen.

Oops, Did I Cross the Line?
John 6:1-15

There are two words that really seemed to me to be lifted up as important for both of these passages of Scripture. These words are abundance and scarcity. In today's world and probably the world that came before us, and in the world that will come after us, scarcity really seems to be how we function. We function with this notion that it is the truth that scarcity exists.

Actually, we do have a tendency to teach our children that and we raise them up with that sort of mindset. Maybe you're experiencing it now with your child or you have raised your children and you see this example. A child wants to play on a sports team, but you find out the sports team only has a certain number of positions and your child is not good enough to make the team. Do they make the team? Probably not. Maybe you are preparing to audition for one of the symphonies in New York as a child and you discover that there are only a certain number of chairs. Not everyone will be accepted and if you don't play well enough, you probably won't be playing with the symphony.

I think many of you may have experienced this sort of thing in life. I must say I have dreams that still haunt me from when I was a child. Kids split up to make two teams to play some games, some sports game. You have the team captains and they're picking the teams. How many of you were the last one picked to be on the team? This idea of scarcity and how we live with it and learn it when we grow up doesn't stop with just the childhood games and the childhood activities. Even as you are preparing for college, you discover that colleges only want to take the best.

They only want the ones who have the best grades, the ones who have the best resumes. If you don't meet those standards, do you make it into college? No, you don't. This world that we live in functions with this as the truth; that this truth of scarcity is something you're living now. I wonder how God defines what abundance and scarcity is? Would God's definition look different than the world's? It's easy for us to buy into the world's definition of scarcity because we see all around us that the economy is failing, jobs are being lost, and we want the protection of our nation. We have this way of closing ourselves in and hoarding for ourselves because we have fear that there will not be enough resources or energy. It doesn't matter, we're not going to let go of what we have.

I would say God's definition flies in the face of the world. It is the truth of abundance and the abundance of God ought to be our bed rock and help us recognize how the myth of scarcity can have its hold on us. I wonder what causes us to really get so fearful and to mistrust that God is a God of abundance. God has proven that he is a God of abundance time and time again from the time of creation, from the way God provided for the Israelites in the exodus, the way that God continues to provide for us in God's salvation in Christ, and how God will continue to provide for us in the future. That is the truth that God is the one who blesses us with abundance! Here, we have the story of David, who God had blessed, who God had empowered, who God had given authority to be the king of the people of Israel.

Unfortunately, David got a little bit too comfortable in his position. He saw something he wanted, and he crossed over the line between recognizing the abundance of God and how God provides. He crossed over the line and decided to take that which he wanted although it wasn't necessarily what God was providing.

I think, like David, we have a tendency to be motivated either by our desires, our flesh, our pride, our ego, or our fear because if we don't do it, we aren't going to have enough. David stepped over the line and he used his position of power, the power God placed in him, to rationalize that it was okay and that he was entitled. I wonder how often we have a tendency to step in and take what is not necessarily ours to have. Our power that God places in us, we use not for the good of the people but instead we use for own desires, our own satisfaction, and our own achievements.

David realized that he stepped over the line. He took a step further to try to make Bathsheba's pregnancy legal. He went to this pattern of deceit and when that didn't work, he got Uriah drunk. When that didn't work, he only thought he had one step left. That step was to take things so far into his hands that he was willing to commit murder.

He was willing to cover up for what he took. The funny thing is if you read on just a little bit further in chapter twelve, the second Samuel, Nathan the prophet tells David that God says, "why would you do this?" God says, "if you ask me for anything, haven't you seen what I can give you?" "I will be there and why do you feel the need to take it on yourself?" God says, "ask and I will give."

The New Testament passage actually stands in contrast to this passage in second Samuel. David used his power to take what he wanted for his own good, for his own desires, his selfish sort of mindset. On the other hand, Jesus used his power not for his own satisfaction but for the good of the community. He showed them what God's truth of abundance is about.

The blessing in this story is that the disciples are a lot like us because they had a hard time trying to wrap their brains around how this was going to happen. They had been living with Jesus, they had experienced Jesus and what he had to say and the miracles that he did. They should be eyes wide open to who this man is and in the power that resides in him. Yet, they got stuck by the worldly conventions of how things work. Jesus as Scripture tells us that he asked them how are we going to satisfy the physical needs of these people?

The Scripture says this question was to test them because he knew what he was going to do. He wanted to see if the disciples were able to put aside the normal conventions and to see what God's abundance can look like. Like us, the disciples couldn't see it. It would take eight month's wages to buy something that they might get to have a bite of and the loaves and fish might get them a little bit more, but it's still not enough. Why do we continue to have blinders on and not be able to see how the power of God provides the abundance that God offers?

What does God's definition of abundance versus scarcity really look like? I ask the hard question and I want us to think about it for just a moment. Is this place that we're sitting in right now an example of God's abundance? Someone downstairs responded, "well yes and no," and I think that's true. God has indeed blessed us from the beginning of the generation that started this church until now. We can see God's abundance in the scale, the size, and the beauty of the place where we gather together! What if we asked our neighbors that live around our church?

Would they see this place as an example of God's abundance? What if we walked down to W. Market Street and we talked to the family of the little girl who was been killed in a drive-by retaliation shooting because she was trying to protect her brother? What if we just go two to three blocks north or east and we talk to the neighbors that live in this community and struggle with crime, with violence, with drugs, and gangs? This is their daily life when they struggle to survive, to have a roof over their head, and to feed their families. Would those communities look around our church and look at us and say, "yeah, First Pres., now there's God's abundance." The challenge for us is to make that response be yes and it means that we have to be able to ourselves believe in the abundance of God. We have to believe in the truth that God is going to provide so that no matter what time, no matter what season, we are able to be the kingdom of God for the people we sit amongst! This isn't easy work and it causes fear and it causes us to cling to scarcity. Fear can keep us in this place because it's difficult for us to figure out how to be present. I can guarantee you that many of the youth that went on the senior mission trip would be able to say to you, "to be the kingdom of God, to make God's love present, to make God's love known, means that you have to be with the people." "You have to have the children sit on your lap and love them." "You have to engage them and hear their stories." "You have to sit and be in contact with them."

That's out of our comfort zone and it pushes us and challenges us. Do we stay on one side of the line, the line of scarcity or can we actually cross over the line to God's abundance and be the kingdom of God here in this place? Jesus took bread, he broke bread, and then he gave it to the people to eat so that they were satisfied. When they collected everything together, there were twelve baskets full of bread left. It wasn't just about those who were gathered in that moment that were satisfied. It was symbolic for us to realize that God's abundance flows from us to others and calls us to be the sacramental community here in this place.

We have to allow ourselves to be blessed and to be broken. I had some conversation after last worship with a couple of members and they wanted to know how do we begin? It begins with us being willing to step across the line and to believe and trust in the truth of God's abundance. We must be willing to risk our very selves to be present with the strangers among us! It means thinking outside of the box. It means to be like Jesus where Jesus always meets us where we're at. If we expect people to meet us here where we're at, we've already missed it. This is good news because just like God forgave David when he repented of his sin, God remains with us challenging us and encouraging us to live the truth of God's abundance.

God remains with us so that the world may not allow their myth of scarcity to overcome us. Today we baptize, and we remember that we are baptized children of God. We remember that God's abundance, including of us, and God's grace is here. Do you believe it? Do you believe in God's abundance or will the world's myth of scarcity carry us away? Let us baptize and celebrate. Amen.

Keep Your Spit to Yourself of Sense and Sensibilities
Mark 8:14-26

I'm going to assume something about at least most of us here. I'm going to assume that we have a sense of decorum, right? We know how things ought to be, right? We know how to behave in public, right? For instance, we know that it is frowned upon and we wouldn't do something like picking our nose in public, right? We might save that for private but not in public. Perhaps, we might find it appalling to walk out on the street and find somebody urinating outside, right? That is something that our decorum does not allow. In India, it's allowed but not here. We wouldn't go to a restaurant, go to someone else's table, and pull food off their plate and eat it. I think that we probably work very hard to try to be very aware of not speaking things that might be considered offensive and that really go against our sensibilities.

I can almost guarantee that if I spit in your face, you would be absolutely appalled. Well we have our common sense in our sensibilities, which are things that we think ought to be in place. We're like that even in church here on a Sunday morning when we gather together with our sensibilities. For instance, if somebody had come in today with a baby and the baby started howling during worship, I can imagine there are at least a couple of us that would turn and glare at the family. We would also likely think why don't they get that child out of here?

I imagine that if in the middle of my sermon, one of you got up and said, "Amen sister," we would have several people who would think that was out of line. I think that the Holy Spirit is such a sensitive subject that if one of us was so overcome by the Holy Spirit and started flopping in the aisles, I am sure that several of us would think that person is crazy. We would also likely think they must be removed. We have decorum in our worship, sensibilities, yes? I think that if we were honest as we engage in Scripture, we find ourselves admitting that even God can offend our sensibilities. Common sense would say, "could we really embrace a God that shows up in the Scriptures?"

For instance, when we think about Moses being called by God to raise his arms, to part the seas and allow the Egyptians to chase after them and cover them up with water so the Egyptian army is killed, aren't we offended by that God? What about the God that would call Abraham to take his son Isaac and bind him up and sacrifice him? Most of us are uncomfortable with that story. We also possibly have trouble with the God that we see in Jesus behaving in a way that kind of affects what we like to know of our God. In chapter seven in the Gospel of Mark, a Syrophoenician woman comes to Jesus and pleads with him to heal her daughter.

Jesus does something that many people have read and are taken aback that this is our Jesus? What Jesus does is he says to this woman, "you feed the children first, the dogs don't count." He essentially calls this woman a dog and in essence, it's like a racial slur. How could Jesus go to that extreme? Our Jesus who happens to say things that confront us calling us vipers, challenging us on what we can see and hear and not understanding. Even further than that, aren't you just a bit taken aback by Jesus both in chapter seven and in this passage that Jesus would think that the way to heal somebody is to spit in their mouth or eye?

If Jesus came to one of you who had some hearing problems or eyesight problems and he wanted to spit at you, would you embrace that? Our sensibilities, when we think about who God is, get pushed back a little bit because that's not how God ought to work. I think this is part of the mindset that Jesus is getting to when he addresses his disciples in the boat. They have just experienced some amazing things. They have experienced Jesus feeding the multitudes two different times and they have experienced him healing a child who wasn't even in his presence. They have experienced Jesus spitting in someone's mouth and that person being able to speak again. Yet, they have a difficult time understanding and grasping who God is in Christ. It affected their sensibilities.

With that in mind, while floating on the lake with the disciples, Jesus says, "you need to be careful of the yeast of the Pharisees." You see, if you have ever baked bread and have had to put yeast in the dough, you might have a little bit of understanding of what this is about. When you put yeast into the dough, the yeast acts as an agent that kind of deteriorates the dough. Yeast ferments the sugar and flour and it starts to create air bubbles, gas bubbles, in the dough so that it can then rise.

Yeast really is an agent that breaks things down, destroys things in a way. Jesus was saying to the disciples that you have to be careful of that which the Pharisees put out before you that can destroy your faith and destroy what you understand and what you're experiencing of who God is. He says, "be careful of the yeast of the Pharisees," and he challenges us to consider that same challenge. The yeast of the world that we live in or even the yeast that is within ourselves. You have to be careful or it can tear down your faith. Now, I think it is a challenge when we think about all the things in our lives that can indeed be like that yeast that can pull us away.

Jesus calls us to that challenge and you know the funny thing is, in the way that he challenges us, he confronts our sensibilities in doing it. I mean do we like to be told by Jesus that, you know what you don't seem to be able to see or what in the world is wrong with you? I kind of bristle at the fact that Jesus is challenging me. What about you? For me, I sometimes would prefer to say to Jesus, "you know, you stay over there and keep your spit to yourself." I don't want that healing because that means you're challenging me to a new way of thinking or a new way of being and I'm not sure I'm prepared.

How many of you, if you were confronted by Jesus, might respond the same way if he said for this healing to happen, I must spit in your face? What would you do? Would you accept in an appropriate way or would you tell Jesus to keep his spit to himself? It's a difficult world that we're in and we find that there are many things that make it difficult for us to be able to conceive, to perceive, the way God works. Some of us may be in work situations that really weigh on us and yeast that seems to be around can easily pull us down the path of forgetting who God is. Perhaps, you are struggling with friendships or family relationships, and you find that the yeast in yourself is getting in the way of who God is calling you to be in that relationship. Students are face to face with the yeast of the expectations of who they are called to be.

How many times has someone asked you what you're going to be when you grow up? The pressures to find that out can easily lead you astray. We move down that path and it's probably more comfortable to say, "Jesus, keep your spit to yourself." "Don't offend my sense and sensibilities." I think we respond a lot like Joseph's brothers. Here is God working in Joseph, proclaiming salvation that will come to them by the dreams that he gives them. Joseph shares those and instead of hearing what God may be doing, Joseph's brothers respond with anger, jealousy, and hatred. How often do we respond to life in that same way?

I think Jesus in this passage in essence, is confronting how we are spiritually blind or spiritually deaf. I think that many of us can come to this place on Sunday morning and worship our Lord. We can do our devotions and we feel like we are on the right track and we've got it all together. We can feel confident that we don't really have spiritual blindness. I believe we can look at ourselves and be honest and discover that what happened is that Jesus is trying to spit in our eyes to heal us and we are resisting. We're like the blind man who receives healing from Jesus and all we can see is his partial sight. We can see people walking around looking like trees. We have to be continually present with our Lord. We have to be continually doing the work to fight the temptations of the yeast that is around us! We have to be constantly allowing Jesus every moment to actually spit in our face! We have to allow Jesus to move us beyond our comfort zone so that we may truly be spiritually aware, have full eyesight, and only then can we fully understand and begin to see how amazing God is! Only then can we see the way that God engages us and offers love, grace, and excitement!

Only when we have our eyes open, are we able to see who God is calling us to be and what God is calling us to do! It is a lot of work, and a lot of attention must be paid. Our challenge today is what will we do when God confronts our sensibilities? We can get up from this place after the service is over and walk outside and we can be willing to allow God to really heal us, to allow God to spit in our face or we can decide that we don't want to go there. Jesus, keep your spit to yourself. What will you, what will we decide to do? Here's to spit in your eye. Amen.

Is It Really Worth Dying For?
Mathew 21:33-46

The prophet Isaiah; he was speaking to the people of Israel. If we think about the time in particular at this moment that he is speaking, we have to remember they were in Babylonian captivity. They had been hauled out of Jerusalem and hauled into captivity. Isaiah was called to bring words of encouragement and hope. He spoke to them and told them to not dwell on the past. He said, "I am doing a new thing and even if you can't perceive it, it's springing up even now." Isaiah paints the picture that draws them into the exodus moment. You heard it, didn't you?

The seas are parted, they walk along the dry ground, the chariots are coming after them, and then the waters cover them and they live no more. Isaiah was calling them to remember the power of God's salvation and liberation but also challenging them to not get so stuck that they can't see how God might go about salvation, liberation, and redemption in a new way. I think this is part of the heart of the parable in Matthew; that Jesus proclaims to those that are sitting by and God is doing a new thing in what they can't even fathom. You see, chapter twenty-one begins with Jesus's triumphant entry into Jerusalem.

Jesus has made his way in and he has turned his face toward the cross. He has turned his face and his heart over to God, knowing that salvation and liberation will be coming in a week as he is killed. He must've had all of this on his mind, this new thing that God is doing. In the midst of that, the Gospel writer of Matthew pulls on several themes. You see, there are things I think that Jesus places in the middle of this parable. After Jesus arrives in Jerusalem, we hear the story of Jesus waking up in the morning and he's hungry, so he goes to the fig tree. He looks for something to eat and he finds no fig to eat.

This frustrates him, and he curses the fig tree and says, "may you not ever produce anymore fruit," and the tree withers right there. The disciples chase after him and ask, "how is this possible?" Jesus says, "if you have faith, you can tell the mountain to go jump into the sea and it will." Jesus was tying fruit and faith and how it gets wrapped up in this parable. In the parable right before this parable, Jesus tells a story. He says, "there is a father who goes to his son and he says to his son, 'I want you go out into the field and work.' The son says no but then he changes his mind and he goes to the field and works.

The father then asks another of his sons to go work in the field and the son says yes but he ends up not going." Jesus asks those who are listening, "who does the father's will?" They respond, "the one who went out to the field." Jesus says, "yes, those who claim that they are people of faith and yet don't take action on it, aren't doing the will of the Father." He says, "they are basically functional atheists." Jesus pulls on this aspect of fruit and faith, and how our actions become part of the whole package. Jesus tells this parable and he says, "we've got this absentee land owner, tenants, servants who are killed, and the son who is killed."

We say, we know this story. The landowner is God, the tenants are the leaders of Israel, the servants are the prophets who were killed, and the son is Jesus Christ. Many of us as Christians could say, why is this really an important piece for us in this day? As far as I know, none of us sitting here are Jewish, Pharisees, or Sadducees. We don't necessarily want to consider ourselves leaders of the church except for us of those that are pastors, elders, and deacons. I think that as we listen, and we try to find ourselves in the story, we are perhaps like the tenants after all. We are leaders whether we choose to embrace it or not because most of us sitting here have been baptized. Our baptism makes the statement that we are dead to ourselves and that Jesus Christ is the ruler and so therefore we put ourselves in the position to be people that lead in the faith. That might be too scary for some of us, so we think that we're just hanging out, listening to Jesus.

Those who would be sitting, listening to this parable, would probably side with the tenants because the idea that an absentee landowner who wants us to do the work and then wants to reap our harvest isn't favorable. The people listening to this parable would think the tenants are doing a good job and taking ownership of what is theirs! How often do we find ourselves in that same position and forgetting who is really the one who owns it? Jesus says, "don't side so quickly with the tenants because they weren't recognizing who God is and what they were to be providing."

He says to those who were listening, "you were given the kingdom and invited to be a partner in this ministry of God's kingdom to bear fruit." "If you can't bear fruit, if you're like the fig tree that isn't producing, God will take the kingdom from you and will give it to someone who can produce fruit!" It's not an easy place to be and if we're honest, it confronts us today, about how we live our lives. So often, we do function as functional atheists and we're like the son who was asked to go to the field and didn't go. We claim we're Christian, yet we don't apply God's Word and we let go of God's Word.

I was reading *Unfashionable*, which was written by the grandson of Billy Graham, and he tells about a friend that he visits, and they often have great theological conversation. His friend says, "you Christians always talk about using the Bible as your standard for everything." "Your guide to the way you live." "I mean seriously, what's your fascination with that outdated book?" "I told him Christians aren't the only people who use standards to govern their lives." "Everyone does it." "Everyone appeals to some authority when determining how to navigate their lives." His friend says, "not me." The grandson of Billy Graham says this, "answer me this, how do you decide between right and wrong?" "How do you decide between good and bad?" "How do you decide between what might move you forward and what might move you back?" His friend says to him, "I use my gut." "I use my instinct." "I certainly don't need an antiquated book to help me do it."

The grandson of Billy Graham says, "so it's not that I govern my life according to a standard while you don't." "Apparently, the difference is that you are serving your own standard." "You are your own authority while I appeal to the Bible as mine." So often, we're put in positions and really don't take the Word of God that God has given us and apply it. I imagine if we're honest, we're using our own authority instead of God's Word. Jesus challenges the Pharisees, the Sadducees, the listeners, and us to bear fruit because God comes to the fig tree and is hungry for righteousness, and if he finds no fruit, surely, we will be cursed. Jesus challenges us to grab a hold of the kingdom that God has placed in our hands and to live faithfully with courage and with strength. This leads me to the question for today.

Is it really worth dying for? Is applying our faith and using God's Word to help us make choices of how we interact with each other in the world, is that really worth dying for? There are really two journeys you can take. You can answer that from the point of view from is it worth neglecting our faith and not really engaging what we believe because if we choose that path, Christ is clear. He says to them, "the stone which he is the stone." If we reject him and if we're partially Christian and partially atheist, that stone on whom it falls will be crushed.

Is it really worth dying for to take the easier road? There's also the other track. Is it really worth dying for? We've been baptized into the death and resurrection of Jesus Christ and made promises that we will die to ourselves and will be guided by our Lord and Savior! Is that path really worth dying for? We may stumble and have broken bones in the process because of rejection that comes from making hard decisions grounded in the Word. We may end up broken but most certainly not crushed. God's salvation and God's kingdom is in our hands and Isaiah and Jesus remind us of the new things that God is doing. Although he knows we're weary with our sins, God says, "I am still the one who redeems, blocks out transgression, and saves."

Do we really believe that? If we really believe that God is the one who saves, then which path we take from is it really worth dying for is clear. Is it really worth dying for? Amen.

Put Your Left Foot In,
Your Left Foot Out
Luke 4:1-13

Testing; we all have had our moments in one form or another with this lovely theme of testing. Whether it's in school and the tests that you must take or whether it's an aspect of diving into a pool. How many of you, thinking about getting into the water, take your toe to test the water out to see if it's the right temperature before you plunge in? How many of you may have taken up the art of ironing and you have decided that you want to make sure that it's hot, so you wet your fingers and smack it to see if it sizzles? A little dangerous but still an aspect of testing. Perhaps, you are one who tests in culinary delights and you take a spoonful of soup and blow on it before taking a spoonful to see if it's a temperature that you're willing to consume.

I'm sure a lot of women are like me when we get dressed in the morning and we put on our outfit to see if we like what we see. Are we too fat? Does our bottom hang out too much? It's a form of testing. We are trying to see if we like what we have in front of us. We're familiar with testing, and today we get to have some time with God and hear how God also likes to test us. This story of Abraham and the story of Jesus will center on this subject of testing and sacrifice.

It's a very fascinating journey. Jesus and Abraham both are placed in a position to live out their faith to make decisions, to make choices about what they really believe, what they really trust in God to do and is God going to actually live into his promises to us? We are to be the bearers of promise just as Abraham and Jesus. Are we worthy of carrying the promises into the future? How does this testing take shape? Well, one thing I think is very interesting and very clear in both of these stories of Abraham and Jesus is it's about the journey. It's not something that necessarily happens in one split moment. It is about the journey that we take, and both of these stories locate this journey in the desert and in the wilderness. Abraham had to journey three days and Jesus forty days in the wilderness. It is about the journey because with Abraham, if it was about whether or not Abraham was willing to sacrifice Isaac, God could have said, "I see that you're about to go on this journey." "I see that you are prepared and it's all over." "We will go about this a different way," but God does not let Abraham off the hook.

It's about the willingness to go through the desert, to the wilderness journey to be continually faithful and trusting that God will provide. The journey is so imperative to us embracing this testing. How many of you are like me when it comes to the wilderness testing and you aren't exactly sure you want to venture out on that? Instead we like to stand on the edge of the wilderness, on the edge of the desert and dip our toe in a little bit and see how the sand is. To actually journey out is scary.

I liken it to "The Hokey Pokey." You know, "The Hokey Pokey?" Yes, you put your left foot in and you put your left foot out, you put your left foot in and you shake it all about. You do the "The Hokey Pokey" and you turn yourself around. "The Hokey Pokey" causes laughter but in the end, "The Hokey Pokey" gets us nowhere. We just turn around in circles and shake our hands and that's all the further we get. How many of you, who like me on this Lenten journey of testing, have been standing on the wilderness edge doing "The Hokey Pokey" and getting nowhere?

The testing is part of our faith journey. We find that in the testing we are refined, and we are able to be better equipped to be bearers of the promises that God gives us. God knows that is an aspect of faith that we live into and so it is something that is part of our journey and it happens through our lives. It's interesting to me that whether it is obvious or explicit, whether it's either God or Satan doing the testing, in the end the results are still the same. You see, it is the struggle in these stories that exhibit the struggles between living into all that God has called us to be, and the struggle of our humanness to decide what we might want instead. The stories both lift that up. I imagine that although our Scriptures don't say this about Abraham, this journey that God did not let Abraham off the hook, I imagine that it was an opportunity for Abraham to be tested. Is he going to return back in three days?

Is Abraham willing to remain steadfast in this commitment? Could you imagine Abraham mulling it over as he walks through the desert? "I don't know, I'm having second thoughts about this whole sacrifice thing." Jesus himself, had challenges placed before him. "Do I respond with my power, my pride?" Those are the same things that get in our way and pull us away from all that God has to offer. We have twelve days left before we get to Easter Sunday. What do we do with the time that we have left? Will we remain on the edge of our wilderness or maybe play around in the sand in front of us? Will we have the courage to actually throw ourselves into a head long dive into the desert and give up what God calls us to give up? Sacrifice in the midst of testing is a challenge because we do like to have things in our control.

This testing, this journey means giving up being distracted and doing "The Hokey Pokey" and turning ourselves around and getting nowhere. It means actually engaging, looking at ourselves, and seeing what God is showing us what we need to give up in order for us to be able to embrace the promises to bring those promises alive in the world! What is your Isaac? What is our Isaac as a community of faith that we need to bind up to let go of? You know, in the end, it is all about how we live into our relationships and how we live into our relationship with God! It is about trusting, being present, and it means we will be called to live into our integrity, into our hopefulness, and into risking being hurt!

It is something that we go into this journey not alone. One of the things that became clear was that God does not expect of Abraham or of us, something God is not willing to do himself. God is willing to sacrifice far beyond what we could even imagine. God is willing to commit himself to honoring promises and to providing a way for us. If God does not expect us to sacrifice something he's not willing to sacrifice, the we know we can stand on the promises that all will be good. In the remainder of our Lenten journey, I hope that you will join with me and stop doing "The Hokey Pokey" the rest of the time that we have but we'll venture out into the desert offering up to God, all that gets in our way, offering to God all that which distracts us from what God is desiring for us to see, to know. I believe that only until we're willing to risk, to venture out, only then will we have a firmer grasp on Easter morning of the reality of what God has done. God's promises are sure. Let's risk ourselves in our relationship with God to discover more fully who God calls us to be. "The Hokey Pokey," the wilderness; I pray we will join together on the wilderness journey that we have left so that we may celebrate with joy on Easter morning the promise that death no longer has the final word. Amen.

The "So What" of Easter
John 20:1-17

I recall some fuzzy memories of my childhood around Easter. I remember I would periodically get a new dress for Easter. Did anybody get a new dress for Easter? Maybe a new bonnet or a new hat? I remember those times and it was so exciting to get a new dress or a new outfit. I also remember vaguely having Easter baskets on Easter. Did anybody get Easter baskets with chocolate bunnies? Who's a fan of chocolate bunnies? What else did you find in your Easter basket? Robin's eggs? Cadbury eggs? Did anybody get Peeps?

These are great memories of Easter. We did Easter egg hunts and it was great fun! Easter is kind of a funny event. It's a funny holiday. It's a little odd when we really think about it. I think that what's happened is Easter is this celebration of stuff that makes us happy. Chocolate bunnies, festive colored eggs, and Easter bunnies that we take pictures with are fun things in a fun time. I'll tell you though, as a preacher, it's difficult to face that kind of happiness.

It's very difficult to try to bring an Easter message that competes with how this world celebrates Easter. Easter is a strange event when you think about it. It really isn't just about joy. It is about death. It's walking through the Good Friday moments and recognizing who we are as human beings and how we have participated in what happens on Good Friday. Easter is joyful, but it is also on the fringes of great sadness. For some it may be guilt and for others, Easter is recognition of the lack of Easter really being present in this world. This is what I mean. God did something that was completely new and different!

God did something that completely shook the order of how we live lives and how we understand how this world works! God did something dangerous in the midst of all the happiness and all the fuzzy stuffed animals and chocolate candies! He changed how we understand what God is doing! Do you see what I mean? What I mean is that God raised Jesus from the dead. That is confusing, and we don't really have good, solid answers. It's safer to have chocolate bunnies, bubblegum, and bright colored eggs because it's fun, happy, and easy.

It has the answers and yet Easter itself is filled with complexity and mind-boggling events. This story from the Gospel of John highlights that confusion and challenge. Here is Mary and she is in the midst of intolerable, unfathomable grief. The loss that she must have been feeling from the death of the one she thought was going to be the one to save them. How can Jesus be dead? She gets up before the light has even risen and she goes to his tomb so that she can have a moment with him to cry and grieve. It is in the darkness that she comes to that tomb. She gets there, and she discovers that he is not there.

You see, we understand God and his creation to work in a certain way. She wasn't expecting that he was actually alive. She was even more heart broken because her Jesus was gone. Somewhere in the dark, someone came and took her Jesus. As the story goes on, the disciples come and do their funny running to the tomb thing. One goes in and one stays out. We don't know what they believe but what we know is that nobody knew where Jesus was. Mary couldn't just sit there so she continued to go into the tomb and cry and try to grasp what has happened. The angels show up and they're sitting there and asking, "why are you crying?" Mary tells them that she has come for her Jesus. Jesus shows up and she doesn't recognize him, and she thinks he's the gardener. He finally calls her by her name and it finally dawns on her that Jesus is alive. I wonder if today, do we really have a knowledge, an awareness, a deep understanding of what Easter is truly about. We are a funny people, right? Every year, we talk about Jesus's advent, his birth, and we go through the process of Lent and going into the wilderness with Jesus and we celebrate how he is risen after Good Friday. Do we know why though?

Easter that first Easter morning over two-thousand years ago, God did something mind-boggling. He did a new thing and he showed for us what he's all about. It isn't about us feeling guilty about our sins and trudging them along in a big backpack through life. God showed us that he has the capacity to release us from the backpack of sin. God wants us to liberated and free and to live in this life as new creations. This thing that he started in Genesis, the magnitude, the fulfillment of that, went all through our story to this time on Easter morning when God shows he can bring life out of death. We celebrate it every year and I ask why? What is the "so what" of Easter? Why do we do it every year? He's already risen! Someone answered, "to give thanks" and that's a possibility, but I think it's even more than that and this is what I mean. How many of you live lives as Easter people, as new creations, who never, ever, ever, ever get bogged down in the darkness of your life? Anyone? The darkness of this life. People, we come to this place on Easter morning in the midst of darkness because it is the life that we actually lead.

We live lives full of grief because mothers, fathers, children, and grandchildren die. We come in this darkness because there are those of us that struggle with addiction. It doesn't matter what kind of addiction; alcohol, drugs, sex, or food. We have people that live in the darkness of mental illness that struggle to find any sense of joy because they're just so troubled inside. We have people sitting in this congregation today who can say that because of the color of the skin, they have to live life differently. They have to teach their children to respect the law because they may be taken to a darker place just because of the color of their skin. Has Easter come for them? We live in a dark world where we know that children, boys, girls, men, and women are trapped in sex trafficking. We live in a world where ethnic cleansing goes on way over there and here. We live in a world where terrorists can blow up buildings and shoot people. We live in a world where teenagers feel a need to go into schools and shoot kids. Has Easter come? Has Easter come? The reason that I think we do this season of Christ's birth, death, and resurrection is because we have to constantly remind ourselves that even in the darkness that we live in, the struggles and disappointments that are part of our lives, we have to remember that God still is in control.

The "so what" of Easter is that even in the midst of our hurt, suffering, and pain, God has shown us that he can do a new thing! God has shown us that he is in control and that he brings new life! The question for us is will we live into our Easter people identity? We might do it the rest of today, tomorrow, and if we're really conscientious, maybe for a week. Life happens though, and someone might lose a job or have a death of a family member. Someone may have someone dear to them fall back into depression. Some of us have to pay bills, do dishes, do laundry, and shovel the snow if we get snow today. Life happens and soon we'll be back into the hum drum of our darkness but no fear! Next year we come back and celebrate Easter again to remind us what God does and calls us to. The "so what" of Easter is for us to really try hard to be okay with the fact that we may be broken people, but God loves us anyway. God came and broke into this world in a little tiny baby and left this world taking with him, us. There is great joy! It isn't that we say he is risen! We say it, but we don't always necessarily believe it. He is risen! He is risen indeed! If he is indeed risen, we have a sure and certain hope that this darkness that we live in will never, ever, ever be able to consume us because his light shines in us. The Gospel of John starts with this imagery of darkness and light. Mary comes in the dark but in that dark, the light of Jesus is shining. Brothers and sisters, I challenge us all, me too, to work harder to live as Easter people. I hope that when the darkness starts to consume us we remember that we are Easter people. We are people of a God who conquers death and does new things all the time. When we come to next Easter, maybe we can say we are a little closer this year to living as Easter people and showing the world what the "so what" of

Easter is all about. He is risen. He is risen indeed. Praise be to God. Amen.

Crying Stones
Luke 19:29-40

Who likes a good parade? Any of you like a good celebration? I know that there was a celebration about three years ago that was very popular here in Kansas City. The Royals! Wave your palm branches! They won the World Series, and everyone came out in droves and celebrated the Royals! I remember pictures and seeing all the blue in front of Union Station. We in Kansas City like a good party, celebration, and parade and we know how to do it well. There's proof! I wonder if Jesus were to arrive right now in front of our church, would there be the same celebration, the same hosannas shouted in honor of the crowning of a king? What do you think? Do you think lots of people would come out to celebrate Jesus? Maybe?

Do you think the number of people would be as large as the number of people that celebrated the Royals winning the World Series? Probably not. It is a tricky thing to be wrapped up in celebration and Psalm Sunday is no exception. It does beg the question of what moves us? What brings us to tears or to celebration? What brings us to a place of warm feelings or a sense of awe?

On Friday, I was waiting to have lunch with my mentor at the First Watch in North Kansas City. As I was waiting, I saw an older gentleman and his wife. He was using a walker and before I could open the door for the gentleman, a young teenage boy opened the door for the man. In this age when we say that teenagers don't have respect for others, I was moved. I was caught by this act of this young teenager opening the door for this older gentleman. It's the little things that catch us and bring us to tears. I had another event about a week ago.

My family and I went to the Art of the Brick. Have any of you been to this art display? I really encourage you all to go. It's an art display of different art pieces put together by Lego bricks. As I moved through this art, I was moved and brought to goosebumps when I saw this display of blue Legos of a woman swimming. It's as if it's taken from the top so you only see the top half of the woman's body on top of the water.

It really moved me and ignited my imagination and it challenged me to think about what we see and don't see. As I moved through the display, I saw pieces that actually brought me to tears. One of the pieces was of a person in red Legos, standing and trying to move forward but he had gray hands holding him back. What are they ways that people hold us back and keep us from moving forward? It hit a cord in myself; the ways that I grieve and am challenged from moving forward. It was moving to me because I recognized that I wasn't alone. This artist created things that spoke to my own pain, my own grief, and my own struggles.

It was liberating to know here is an artist creating art and speaking what was in my soul. How many of you are moved when you realize that you aren't alone and that someone understands that place inside you? This celebration, this day that we proclaim is a challenging one in that. You see, the Jews and the disciples that were celebrating and shouting hosannas were looking for a king to liberate them. Not for a way that God knew they needed to be liberated but from the oppressive powers and the way that their lives had been squelched.

They wanted a king to liberate them in order to celebrate what it means to be people of God. They were shouting hosanna and waving palm branches and making a way for this one who would change their lives forever! We know that is dangerous. You see, the governor always made a procession in himself. How many of you know about that? That on the Passover, the governor on a processional on a horse with military might would come in. What is the Passover all about for the Jewish people? Freedom and liberation, right? It's a celebration of who God is and how God saved the Hebrew people and liberated them. The Roman government knew that if the Jewish people were left to their own devices, they might get a wild heir and revolt. The Roman governor would make a mighty entrance to keep the order and to remind the people that the Roman government was here.

On the same day that Pilate, the Roman governor, came in the main gate, Jesus came in the back gate on a humble donkey with no military might. He makes an entry that puts another take on what it means to be king. When we get wrapped up in the party and celebration, we think we have a king that's going to save us. The problem that comes with the celebration is this king that we think we want, is the same king that tells us we must pray for our enemies and share everything with others. We must open ourselves up to doing things in a new and different way than the world does. Who wants a king like that?

They didn't and a week later, the same people that were shouting hosannas turned around and did what? They crucified him! We have a tendency to have a disconnect between what we really want and really need. The challenge is to be honest with ourselves about the disconnect that we live every day. The Pharisees who were present as Jesus was entering, told Jesus to tell his people to shut their mouths because it's a dangerous thing to say you're king. They told Jesus, "if you're not careful, they'll put us in jail." Jesus responded, "even if everyone said not a word, the stones would cry out." You see here is Jesus, coming in as king to the shouts of hosannas and praises.

In Luke, they say, "hosanna praise be to the one who brings peace on earth." It's a different peace than Pilate brings across town. Despite the fact that we so often are afraid to shout hosanna and instead shout crucify, Jesus still comes in on a donkey and walks his way to the cross. God is still with us even in our moments of fickleness and our moments of silence. God is still with us even when we should be proclaiming our faith and who God is and what God does for us. Because of who God is and what God knows about us, God is still present. You all have stones in your hands. In the midst of all the political stuff, all the school walkouts, gun arguments, sexism, ageism, racism, and in the midst of all the ways we keep our mouths silent, these stones challenge us as they cry out. They challenge us to what does it mean to really shout hosanna and be part of the kingdom where the king wears the crown of thorns. On this Psalm Sunday, let us be challenged to lay down the stones that might cry out and let us use our voices to speak words of faith, love, justice, and peace. We also know that even if we can't keep the stones from crying out because of our silence, Jesus still comes, and God is still with us. Like the artist, God knows our pain, our brokenness, and Jesus still comes. This morning, we will multi-task during communion, bring your offering and your stones. The stones go on the sand path to the cross as an act of saying this is the starting point of silencing the stones with our own voices. In doing so, we accept the offering of communion and place our own offering in response to God. This is the word of the Lord. Praise be to God. Amen.

Sticks and Stones
Isaiah 43:16-21; John 8:1-12

"Liar, liar? Pants on fire!" That's right, you got it! "Tom and Nicole sitting in a tree?" "K-i-s-s-i-n-g!" That's right! "I'm rubber and you're glue, whatever you say?" "Bounces off me and sticks on you!" Yeah! You guys know these! How about this one? "Sticks and stones break my bones but?" "Words will never hurt me!" Yes, yes, yes, we're all familiar with these. It's really quite a shame, isn't it? These childhood songs we're all familiar with and these songs come with a certain level of pain.

I'll never forget a young boy in the fifth grade. I still remember him and his red, curly hair. "Hey Nicky, give me a hickey!" I'm glad some of you find that funny! I on the other hand was mortified! It's not one of your famous playground songs but if anyone calls me Nicky, I have to restrain myself! The things that we say may not be physically dangerous, but they do have an impact. It is all part of the story that we hear in the Gospel of John. If I were to ask you again this week who are you in the story, who are you? Are you the woman who has been caught in sin, dragged out of bed, and brought to Jesus, and announced to the whole community that this woman was caught in adultery? Liar, liar? Pants on fire! Are you this woman, humiliated by what has been revealed and by what the community is thinking?

Are you the Pharisees, the Sadducees, the people of the law who actually ripped this woman out of bed and condemned her? You had a hidden agenda and passed judgement and weren't very kind? Who are you in this story? Both. Who are we as a community of faith in this story? Both. There was a saying, and nobody knows who said it but, "Christians are the only army that will attack their own." What an indictment that is! This story in the Gospel of John really challenges us even today. It is about what we say but also a reflection of what we have in our hearts. Psalm 52:1-4;

> *Why do you boast of evil, you mighty hero?*
>   *Why do you boast all day long,*
>   *you who are a disgrace in the eyes of God?*
> *You who practice deceit,*
>   *your tongue plots destruction;*
>   *it is like a sharpened razor.*
>
> *You love evil rather than good,*
>   *falsehood rather than speaking the truth.*
>
> *You love every harmful word,*
>   *you deceitful tongue!*

There are many Scriptures that warn people of faith of things that the tongue can do, the words that people say. In the end, what God gets at is that the things that we say are the reflection of what's in our hearts and spirits. This story is about the woman who was caught in adultery and she was a sinner but here are these men that are working out of deceit in their hearts. They aren't working to bring about justice because if they were, they would have brought both the man and the woman before Jesus. They humiliate the woman before the crowd.

They weren't about the law. They were about trapping Jesus. They knew if he said, "we need to stone her because that's what the law says," he would have been arrested by the Romans because the Jews had no authority to enact civil justice! They knew that if Jesus said, "it's okay, there's no judgement," they were able to say that, "he's not a real Jew and that he doesn't follow the law!" They didn't care about the woman or the law. They were all about their own agendas and that they could get rid of Jesus.

I wonder what it was that Jesus wrote in the sand. Jesus said, "whoever is without sin, they can cast the first stone." Then he bent down and wrote in the sand some more. He must've written something very profound, something that the Pharisees and Sadducees knew that he was calling them out on. You see, he wasn't talking about who was condemnable. He was really turning the tables on them and he was asking who was in a position to condemn?

He was asking who was in a position to pick up the stones and throw because by the Jewish law, the person had to have another witness. Those two witnesses were in a position to cast the first judgement. He was saying, "maybe you should reflect on Scriptures." What he wrote in the sand caused them to recognize that if you say so and have committed a sin, you had better not have committed the same sin yourself.

Jesus was not saying to get rid of judgement but to contemplate who is actually in a position to condemn and the only answer is God. It begs the question who are we in the story? I think we are both of those parties because we have all been in a position where someone has made us feel worthless and like we are about to be stoned. I know I have but I also know that in my heart, I have picked up a stone out of anger, frustration, envy, jealousy, pride, and I wanted to cast stones. How many of you, like me, wanted pain to befall someone else? I know I have.

We have all been in those positions where we have felt vulnerable, broken, and ashamed. We've been in positions where we've picked stones up. Sticks and stones may break my bones, but words will never hurt me is actually a falsehood. In a book that someone was writing about CS Lewis, he was at a conference on comparative religion and they were all trying to figure out what made Christianity different than other religions? CS Lewis walked in on this discussion and he said, "grace is what makes it different." Here is this woman in the story, and she was a sinner and caught in the act of adultery.

Yet, when she deserved to be stoned because that was the law, Jesus wouldn't go there. Jesus's grace and openness, wrapped her up and gave her words of comfort, not words of harm. He gave her and gives us, unmerited grace.

Something that is not deserved, not earned and something we can't buy at the store; grace. In this world of massacres, school shootings, sexism, racism, ageism, etc., there is one religion that has the capacity to drop the stones, to not pass judgement, to love, embrace, and to enfold others with grace. The question for us today is are we courageous enough to drop those stones and accept grace, share grace, and start making a difference in this world of non-grace? Are we courageous enough to stop being the Christian army that would turn on its own soldiers and start showing the world that God loves us beyond imagination? We can start showing how God is doing a new thing in our community, neighborhoods, and in our world. The challenge today, as you hold that stone, and to have the courage to place it on the path to the cross and really mean to drop it. Amen.

Botanical Carnage
Psalm 22:25-31; John 15:1-8

We have Mark Davis's translation from Greek to English and the NIV translation. There's some slight variations because of how the Greek language can be translated and the semantic ranges in that. This is the Gospel of John, 15:1-8;

I am the true vine, and my Father is the gardener. He cuts off every branch in me that bears no fruit, while every branch that does bear fruit he prunes so that it will be even more fruitful. You are already clean because of the word I have spoken to you. Remain in me, as I also remain in you. No branch can bear fruit by itself; it must remain in the vine. Neither can you bear fruit unless you remain in me.

I am the vine; you are the branches. If you remain in me and I in you, you will bear much fruit; apart from me you can do nothing. If you do not remain in me, you are like a branch that is thrown away and withers; such branches are picked up, thrown into the fire and burned. If you remain in me and my words remain in you, ask whatever you wish, and it will be done for you. This is to my Father's glory, that you bear much fruit, showing yourselves to be my disciples.

We as human beings, we love carnage. We do. How many of you when you're driving down the road and you see a major car accident, love to be those people that slow down and look to see what kind of destruction there is? Yes, come on admit it. We love to rubberneck because we love to see metal carnage ripped up. If we happen to see blood and guts, so be it, but we love the metal carnage. It's not just driving by accidents that we love.

In North America, since film has been in its inception, the one theme that has consistently been on the rise of popularity is what? Action and superhero films. People love the action, the carnage, the destruction. You know I'm right. There's another kind of carnage that we experience in the spring; botanical carnage. How many of you have been out in the garden clipping, pruning, and cleaning up the botanical carnage? I know my mom has been and my dad has been cleaning up the botanical carnage. We love carnage. What's funny about this passage is if you notice the nuances between the Mark Davis version and the NIV version, you see slight variations in the Greek. What happens is the translators, somewhere deep down inside them, love the carnage too.

This passage when read in the NIV translation is kind of scary and really lives out the botanical carnage. I read this translation and tweaked it a little bit because the Greek is a little bit softer and not as scary. This idea of botanical carnage that we see in this passage is softened when we think about some of the dynamics of being a vine dresser. Now, when I was first called into ministry, the first church I took was in Alton, Illinois. The family that we stayed with until we could find a house had a vineyard.

My family and I had an opportunity to work in the vineyard. It really was an interesting thing to be hands on with. It caused me to look more into the vine dressing, grape producing, horticulture aspect because it speaks a lot to who we are as people of faith. The vine imagery and grapes turn into wine, right? In verse two, "every branch in me that does not bear fruit, he lifts up."

The reason why that is an interesting translation is because the Greek word that often gets translated as removed or cut off actually can be translated as lifts up. This is important when you put vine dressing in the mix of this. If you're growing a vineyard, when your branches are growing off of the vine and they aren't tended to, the branches grow on the ground. When the branches grow on the ground, they want to put roots in the soil.

When that happens, the vines aren't producing anything deep and the grapes that are grown are usually small and bitter. A vine dresser comes along and lifts those branches that aren't bearing much fruit and ties them to a trellis. A vine dresser has to intentionally raise those branches up and tie them to a trellis, so they are forced to draw their nutrients from the main vine that is deep in the ground. The NIV wants to translate that Greek word in a nasty way and the writer of the Gospel of John takes that word and leans into the idea of vine dressing and knowing that God is a God of love. God isn't the one who's going to lop off an arm or a leg just because it isn't producing fruit. God takes those branches and lifts them up and gives them a second chance. When those branches are really producing good fruit and abiding in the vine, the vine dresser prunes those branches so that the vine and the branches can be more productive. They're spending their energy on one thing instead of having branches growing every which way.

This is the kind of God who we are called by Jesus to abide in, dwell in, and to remain in. This is the God of second chances that desires for us to be living, thriving, and loving. Now, where this imagery kind of breaks down is that the vine and the branches don't have a choice in the matter. We do. We have the choice to decide whether or not to abide in the vine. Whether we aren't producing fruit yet or are producing lots of fruit, we still choose to abide. The funny thing about this passage is that we have a way that the producing of the fruit is all of our doing. That we are the ones that if we do good works, we're producing good fruit. We are a country of producers. We get our worth by what we produce and how well we produce it. If we think about it, we think people living in poverty, homelessness, and on welfare, are non-productive members of society. I wanted to share a quote with you.

How many of you have seen *Say Anything?* It's about a young man named Lloyd Dobler who is trying to find his way and he falls in love with a girl. Lloyd is invited to have dinner with the girl and her father. The father asks Lloyd, "what are you going to do with your life, Lloyd?" Lloyd responds, "I don't want to sell anything bought or processed, or buy anything sold or processed, or process anything sold, bought, or processed, or repair anything sold, bought, or processed." "You know as a career, I don't want to do that." That's a great answer, right? He resists this element of our culture that is all about producing. This passage challenges that thought because we don't produce good fruit because of the good work that we do. We cannot good work ourselves into salvation and we cannot good work ourselves into showing the world that we have good fruits. This passage challenges us to recognize that it is God who is supplying the nutrients and is involved in producing that in us. We must be abiding in order for that to happen.

It's a challenge because abiding in the vine means moving ourselves out of the way, letting God's Word fill us. The messy part of the NIV translation of "if you abide in me and my words abide in you, whatever you determine is required will come into being for you all." That passage is basically saying that all that abiding gets us is our wishes and God is the magical wish granter.

The Greek translation is deeper and says if we are abiding, the things that we actually are wishing for is recognizing what is needed in this world. It has nothing to do with us but is about knowing what God wants is granted. Do you all see the difference? In the Greek translation of verse seven, "if you all abide in me and my words abide in you all, whatever you may determine is required, it will come into being for you all." This translation uses the plural form, and this is significant because Jesus is saying, "listen, you don't get to live on the vine as individuals!" "You have to recognize the importance of abiding in me and the communal aspect of you all abide in me, it will be seen in you all!"

The community aspect of what we do is so important. We must abide in Christ together and it means that there is a lot of risk involved because it means sharing our lives together. The writer of John made it clear that all of this centered on sacrificial love. Jesus is basically saying if you are abiding in the Father, in the vine, and loving each other, and you will make that known as a community. That brothers and sisters is scary stuff. I think God has brought a beautiful community together and has done great beginning things here but I think it is time to deepen our abiding. We need to allow God to lift us up off the ground and tie us to the trellis and allow us to blossom and allow fruit to be born in us. It's a matter of setting aside what we want and wish and really listening to what God is calling us to be. God is calling us to be a community that loves one another, loves others and everything we do. As we move forward and have these Rethink conversations, I invite you to come and grow as we abide and see how God is producing fruit in us. Let's allow God to prune us and clean us together so that we may be even more fruitful together. Praise be to God. Amen.

#Dirty Four-Letter Word of The Gospel
John 15:9-17;1 Corinthians 13:3-8; Psalm 63:1-5

When I was younger, I had a habit of hanging on to things. Actually, when I was in high school, I had made kind of a wall hanging over my bed. I put things on this wall hanging like the tickets to concerts that I went to, corsages from dances that I went to, and flowers from guys that took me to dances. I had all kinds of memorabilia and my parents went to Paris and they brought me back a beret and I put that up too. It was a matter of keeping those memories, those things, close to me.

Do any of you still hold on to things like that? It's a way for us to remain connected to those things that, whether we are aware of it or not, they shape our identity. It connects us to a place in this world and shapes us and reminds us of who we are and where we come from. Now, I actually took that wall hanging down and unpinned all of those things. Most of that stuff did probably get thrown away but I still have some things that I hold on to. One of those things is this pair of overalls I'm wearing today. I pulled these out and these are actually my mom's father's overalls.

Grandpa Jess was his name, and he was a farmer in Texas and he wore a pair of these overalls practically every day of the week. He was outside a lot and he loved these overalls. Out of all the things that I have from my grandpa, this pair of overalls really connects me to him. It reminds me of my identity and the stuff that I'm made up of because my Grandpa Jess was a man of integrity. Although, he only had a seventh-grade education, he was so very wise and he was a hard worker. He loved his family and he showed me what it meant to be connected to the earth and to be connected to creation. With this pair of overalls, I'm connected to him and all those things that he stood for. It's part of my identity and so I wear these today proudly.

This passage in the Gospel of John is a passage for us today that connects us to our identities. This is the whole piece of the Gospel of John and it is really Jesus's words and proclamation and teaching the disciples about who to be, what they are called to be, and helping to answer questions connecting them to their identity. This is after the Lord's Supper. This is after he had washed the disciples' feet and he showed them what it means to humble oneself. He's saying these words because he knows he is not going to be with them for much longer in the way that they know him to be.

These are his words to help shape their understanding of who they are and who we are as people of faith. These words follow what we learned last week, and he is calling us to remember to love, to abide in him, and he who abides in God and the life force of love flows through him. When he says, "when you abide in that, you are living love.' He goes on to say, "I share this with you, I share my life with you in such a deep and intimate way because I no longer call you servants." "I call you friends."

This is so profound brothers and sisters, because as servants, you just do what you're told to do! As servants, you don't really have a choice in the matter to know what the master is doing, and you just do what you're told. You don't get to be in relationship with the master when you are a servant. Jesus said "I call you friends, not acquaintances, not people that I visit once a year. I call you friends." This identity of being called friends is profound because it calls us to a relationship that is so very, very personal, so very intimate where God through Jesus knows us, but we are invited to know him. You see, love is really a dirty four-letter word. I'm sure if I gave you a moment to think of dirty four-letter words, you all could come up with one or two. Crap is one and I won't go any further.

Love is a four-letter word; it is a four-letter word of our Gospel and the reason that it's a dirty word is because in reality, the deep meaning, the profound nature of love is not an easy one and it's actually kind of scary. We toss the word love around pretty free handed; I love pizza, I love scuba. What do you love? Golf, tennis, judo, shopping. We love these things. We toss around the word love so much that in honesty, it doesn't have the depth and doesn't reveal the scary nature of this word. This word, love, is about so much more than warm and fuzzy's, chocolates, and bunnies. The love that comes when we abide in Christ is a love that is sacrificial. It is a love that calls us to not think of ourselves but to think of others. It's not about compromise.

I think that compromise is an awful word because compromise, particularly when we're in relationship with one another, ultimately and suddenly starts to build up resentment. Love on the other hand, love is about the other. It's one of the reasons why God didn't say compromise with each other but "to love as I have loved you." That means we had the cross sitting at the center of that statement. It is a cross that Jesus shows us what it means to sacrifice. We have plenty of Scripture that points to that and gives the description of this love that we are called to share. If we really are in an intimate, personal relationship with Jesus, this is the love we are called to share with other people. This is from first Corinthians chapter thirteen;

If I give everything I own to the poor and even go to the stake to be burned as a martyr, but I don't love, I've gotten nowhere. So, no matter what I say, what I believe, and what I do, I'm bankrupt without love.

Love never gives up.
Love cares more for others than for self.
Love doesn't want what it doesn't have.
Love doesn't strut,
Doesn't have a swelled head,
Doesn't force itself on others,
Isn't always "me first,"
Doesn't fly off the handle,
Doesn't keep score of the sins of others,
Doesn't revel when others grovel,
Takes pleasure in the flowering of truth,
Puts up with anything,
Trusts God always,

Always looks for the best,
Never looks back,
But keeps going to the end.

Love never dies.

Brothers and sisters, to live that love out in this world in this time is scary and risky because it means that we actually have to think and be love. It's a dirty little word of the Gospel but folks, it is so important. It is about this relationship that we continue to say we have as we abide in and allow that love of God to flow through us. The psalmist talks about that intimacy a lot but here's one instance. Psalm 63:1-5;

> *You, God, are my God,*
> *earnestly I seek you;*
> *I thirst for you,*
> *my whole being longs for you,*
> *in a dry and parched land*
> *where there is no water.*
>
> *I have seen you in the sanctuary*
> *and beheld your power and your glory.*
> *Because your love is better than life,*
> *my lips will glorify you.*
> *I will praise you as long as I live,*
> *and in your name I will lift up my hands.*
> *I will be fully satisfied as with the richest of foods;*
> *with singing lips my mouth will praise you.*

The psalmist calls us to recognize that if we are really abiding in what Jesus calls us to and if we're really rooted in this hunger and thirst for God, this intimacy of being known, being revealed, and they are in turn called us to be known and reveal to each other, there we are love. There we will be experiencing joy. Jesus says, "I call you friends," he says, "I have called you, I have claimed you." "I have called you out and appointed you to live out being loved." Let us be the dirty little word of the Gospel in this world. We come to this table so that we know how deeply, how intimately God loves us and gives us a profound identity. May we come to this table and leave being love in this world. Praise be to God. Amen.

www.ingramcontent.com/pod-product-compliance
Lightning Source LLC
Chambersburg PA
CBHW071016120626
46546CB00003B/1116